By
Kathleen Hamilton Eschner
and
Nancy G. Nelson

Group Books
Loveland, Colorado

Drugs, God & Me

Credits
Edited by Nancy M. Shaw
Designed by Judy Atwood
Cover design by Jan Aufdemberge
Cover photo by Jeff Buehler

ISBN 0931-529-41-7
Printed in the United States of America

Dedication

This book is for everyone who's been a child and confronted with uncertain feelings about self, self with peers, self with alcohol and drugs, and self within the family.

This book is dedicated to young people and men and women in all walks of life who've struggled with the disease of chemical dependency. And it's prayerfully hoped that there'll be a way to protect new generations of young people against walking this pain-filled pathway.

This book is dedicated to the men and women in all walks of life who've anonymously gathered in recovery groups and realized that recovery was first and foremost a spiritual experience, as was this book.

This book is dedicated to every person who's working to create alternatives for young people to choose in place of the alcohol and drugs that result in a loss of life and health. May God guide and direct us all.

Acknowledgments

We're grateful to the people and organizations that brought this book from prayerful hope to reality. This book was written under the auspices of Lutheran Social Services of Colorado whose executive director, Chet Evenson, shepherded the agency's commitment to the prevention of chemical illness.

Richard Jespersen, with empathy and professional skill, contributed the vision to develop this project. John Califf communicated a prevention proposal to the Wheat Ridge Foundation of Chicago, which provided financial support to develop the program. Kathleen Hamilton Eshner and Nancy G. Nelson as authors put their knowledge and experiences into lesson plans, which they field-tested and refined with young people and their parents.

For over three years, members of an advisory council—Rev. David Debord, Ms. Nanci Rinehart, Rev. Mark Trechock, Bob Crump, Rev. John Elmshauser, Cindy Kraft, Rev. Steve Dreher and Earl McKinstry—volunteered many hours of shared creativity to help the authors pilot this project in dozens of churches and schools.

Betty Robbins and Mary Hunt, untiring support staff, received stacks of assorted typed and handwritten manuscript pages and used typewriters and computers to make them organized and readable.

Steve Massie maintained communication pathways between these individuals and the offices of Group Publishing.

To all these men and women who became a moving force in unity, we say, "Praise be unto our Father for each of them."

Lutheran Social Services of Colorado

Contents

Introduction

Drugs, God & Me is a response to the intense concern about young people and drug abuse in today's society. This course is designed for ministers, youth workers, counselors, teachers, principals, parents and junior highers who want to prevent drug abuse among young people. Written from a Christian perspective, this course can be used in churches, private schools or communities. These sessions and retreats target junior high young people and their parents as they struggle to communicate about drugs and understand the effects drugs have on individuals and families. The sessions integrate biblical truths into information about building self-esteem and confronting drug-related issues such as facts about drugs and how drugs affect relationships.

Drugs, God & Me includes:

• eight sessions that progress from developing positive self-esteem to recognizing oneself as an active part of a solution in preventing drug abuse.

• handouts that can be photocopied for kids and parents.

• two retreats—one for parents and junior highers together and one for kids only.

• "At-Home Tracks" for each session—to stimulate family discussion and interaction.

Sessions

Leaders can use these sessions a variety of ways, for example:

• weekly meetings for kids only.

• weekly meetings for parents only.

• weekly meetings for parents and kids to meet at the same time with different leaders.

• a weekend retreat, when scheduling time during the week is a problem.

If leaders decide to have the parents and kids meet at different times, one leader can use the Youth or Parent Track with the appropriate group. If, however, leaders decide to have parents and kids meet at the same time, they need two leaders—one to meet with kids in one room and another to meet with parents in a different room. Separating parents and their kids reduces the anxiety level so both groups feel free to talk. Both leaders need a copy of the book and should follow the track they're responsible for. With this format, parents and kids can meet together for the opening and closing activities in most sessions. In Session 7, parents and kids can meet together from beginning to end.

Each session has a unique format. Content is divided into two tracks—an active Youth Track on the left side of the page and an informative Parent Track on the right. When the material for both tracks is the same, the content is printed across the page. Leaders should use the session outline, following the appropriate track. The following example is for a leader who is working with a parent group. He or she will use the content that's indicated by dark type.

Example
Session Activities

Choose the track you want to use. (In this case, the Parent Track.)

Youth Track	Parent Track
total group the group's decision about the person's relationship to the drug.	**Using Drugs Responsibly" as a basis for their discussions.**

When content goes across the page, use this material for both tracks.

8. Chemical health assessment**—Give each participant a photocopy of the "Chemical Health Assessment" handout. Ask individuals to list drugs they know junior highers use and answer the questions about each drug.**

Have individuals talk about their list with the rest of the group and encourage them to answer one another's questions.

Youth Track	Parent Track
9. Closing—Ask participants to form a circle. Give each person a water-based marker. Say: "Each of you has ways you glorify God with your body. On the inside of your palm, write 'I'll glorify God by . . .' and complete the sen-	***9. Closing*****—Give each parent a 3×5 card. Say: "Each of you is aware of ways your junior highers glorify God with their bodies. On this card, write a note to your young person telling how proud you are of**

3. If moderate amounts of caffeine are used in a social setting, nervousness or jittery feelings may not be noticeable. Eating or drinking the same amount of caffeine alone may produce the same physical reaction, but it may be more obvious when no one else is around.

4. Too much caffeine depends upon an individual's tolerance level; however, two 12-ounce colas definitely stimulate the senses.

5. If cola or chocolate is used indiscriminately, sleeplessness or nervousness may occur.

6. Caffeine is legal, readily available and is sometimes a hidden ingredient in foods or beverages.

When material for both tracks begins the page, Youth and Parent Tracks are indicated below.

Youth Track

Have kids choose another drug and discuss the six factors in relation to that drug. Use the information in Session 3 to help them find information they don't know. Encourage group members to discuss how drug use influences family, friends, school, legal responsibilities, finances, work, personal lives and spiritual experiences. Write group members' ideas on the newsprint labeled "The Harmful Consequences of Drug Use."

Parent Track

Have parents meet again in their groups of four. Ask each group to choose a drug besides caffeine and discuss the six factors in relation to that drug. (To make sure each group selects a different drug, ask someone from each small group to let you know what drug the group selected.) Have copies of the drug information from the last session available if parents need it. Encourage parents to discuss how drug use influences family, friends, school, legal responsibilities, finances, work, personal lives and spiritual experiences.

Give each group a sheet of newsprint and markers.

The format of each session:

• **Introduction.** These brief paragraphs explain what each session is about.

• **Notes to the leader.** Some sessions contain material that offers the leader further assistance.

• **Objectives.** These concise statements explain what participants will do and learn.

• **Supplies.** This list tells which supplies are needed for both tracks, unless noted for just one.

• **Preparation.** This section offers detailed guidelines to make the session flow smoothly, and it contains the "Self-esteem booster" (the theme for each session). The first part of Preparation is for both tracks. Special preparations are indicated by "Parent Track only" or "Youth Track only."

• **Session activities.** The session is a series of numbered activities that build on one another. Role plays, handouts, Bible studies, readings and other activities are used to explore the session topic.

"AT-HOME TRACK"

Following each session is an "At-Home Track" designed to stimulate further discussion about the session's content. Leaders should encourage participants to schedule a time for this 30-minute family meeting and see if any questions or concerns result from these additional discussions.

The format of each "At-Home Track":

• Self-esteem booster. This statement repeats the session theme.

• Sharing time. Leaders encourage kids and parents to take materials from the session home to talk about during this time.

• Bible study. Kids and parents read a scripture verse or passage together and discuss what it says to them. They also talk about how they can apply that verse or passage to their lives.

• Activity. This is a time when families can use the session's content to actively do something with what they've talked about. This track may include anything from an opportunity to rate specific feelings and attitudes to taking a hike together.

• A plan of action. A different opportunity is offered each time to continue learning and growing from each session.

RETREATS

The retreats offer an alternative to the weekly meeting approach. A retreat with parents and kids or a retreat with kids only provides a quick way to deal with this subject. During retreats, the "At-Home Track" may be used several ways—after each session, during free time, immediately before "lights out" or as a packet to take home.

No matter which format leaders select, they should encourage attendance since sessions build on one another. All sessions last one hour, although discussion times may vary.

WHY INVOLVE PARENTS?

Drugs, God & Me stresses parental involvement in helping young people avoid drug abuse. Considerable research supports the idea that parents are one of the most influential factors in their young people's lives. For example, in *The Quicksilver Years: The Hopes and Fears of Early Adolescence*, Search Institute reports that in fifth through ninth grades parental influence remains stronger than peer influence.

Parental attitudes and role modeling play an important part in kids' experimentation and drug use. When kids live in alcoholic families, they experience not only the disruption and antagonism of unstable family life, but they see alcohol used as a method to deal with conflict. Healthy family relationships discourage young people's involvement in drug use. Positive family environments nurture self-esteem and contribute to positive choices.

In addition to parental influence, there's concern that genetic factors may also contribute to drug abuse. "Approximately 50 to 75 percent of all clients at alcoholism treatment centers report at least one relative in the preceding two generations who had 'problems with alcohol.' "[1] Therefore, parents should recognize an increased risk when there's a family history of alcoholism.

HOW CAN THE CHURCH HELP?

The church is a healing community. It's a place where people come together for spiritual nurturing. It's a place individuals acknowledge their suffering, estrangement and anxious longing for something better. It's a place people find courage to face their fears and seek a peaceful union with God. Within the Christian community, people learn to embrace life with a creative, hopeful attitude. Spiritual care helps individuals avoid abusing chemicals and heals those recovering from addiction because it offers something that lasts—hope in the midst of pain.

People in the church can help one another gain this hope by doing what they've always tried to do—care for people. Caring for young people means listening to them, taking their concerns seriously and helping them understand their worth in God's eyes. Through this kind of care, kids will begin to realize how much they're loved. Through this kind of care, young people will find hope in the midst of their pain.

[1]Stephanie Griswold-Ezekoye, ed., et. al., *Childhood and Chemical Abuse: Prevention and Intervention* (New York: The Haworth Press, 1986), 56.

SESSION 1

I'm Special Because God Created Me

Positive self-esteem—the value one places upon the self—is an important factor in preventing drug abuse among young people. Junior highers need a positive self-image to meet life's challenges and journey successfully into adulthood.

When young people base their self-image on the knowledge that everyone is created and loved by God, they can affirm themselves. They can say: "I'm special because God created me. God loves me unconditionally. God loves me for the person I am, not because of what I do." When young people realize that each person is special and unique, created in God's image, they see themselves as worthwhile because they're created and loved by God.

This session shows junior highers they're special people who don't need drugs to feel good about themselves. Parents learn how to reinforce this lesson at home.

Notes to the Leader

Today's young people face more personal challenges and social problems than ever before. Recent trends show increased violent crime, suicide, drug abuse and pregnancy among junior highers. Increasing numbers of young people suffer the trauma of parental divorce and live in single-parent homes. As parental influence lessens, peer pressure becomes more intense. Because young people feel they lack family and community support, they move toward their peers to fill an emotional void. They look outside the family for role models to help them identify meaning and purpose in life. With abundant negative media role models, it's not surprising young people are confused about how to develop a healthy lifestyle.

Junior highers want to make personal decisions and define their values, yet they struggle with "Who am I?" and "Where am I going?" To work through these questions successfully, young people need to develop a positive self-image. They need to feel confident, competent and valuable. Only when they value themselves in relation to God, family and friends will they successfully complete the journey into adulthood and maintain a positive, creative outlook.

Why do junior highers have such difficulty feeling valued? One reason they forget they're loved is that adults forget to tell them. Some parents unconsciously express love for what their children do, rather than love them for who they are. They tell them who they shouldn't be, rather than help them find out how they're unique. They tell them what they shouldn't do, rather than discuss with them how to live life to its fullest. They preach about behaviors they're against, rather than support behaviors they approve. They tell their children, "Do as I say, not as I do," instead of modeling behaviors they want to see in their young people.

Parents have numerous opportunities to guide their junior highers toward wholeness and productivity. They can start by helping their kids value themselves. They also can help their kids discover how God is present in everyone's life.

OBJECTIVES

In this session junior highers and parents will:

- learn about their self-image and God's image of them.
- talk about specific ways to build self-esteem.
- promote each other's positive self-image.

SUPPLIES

- ☐ newsprint
- ☐ markers
- ☐ masking tape
- ☐ paper
- ☐ pencils
- ☐ posterboard
- ☐ Bible

"Youth Track" only

- ☐ colored construction paper
- ☐ scissors

PREPARATION

Read the session and photocopy the handouts.

Before the meeting, write the following "Self-esteem booster" on newsprint and tape it onto the wall: "I'm special because God created me and there's no one else like me."

Write the following "Guidelines for Caring" on posterboard and display them at each session. Leave room for additional guidelines at the bottom of the list.

Guidelines for Caring

- Show respect by listening to each person.
- Accept everyone's opinions and feelings as worthwhile.
- Avoid using putdowns, interrupting, name-calling, teasing, laughing, making faces or any behavior that might hurt another person's feelings.
- Share opinions and feelings openly.
- Be concerned about what's best for yourself and others.
- Keep confidential any feelings or personal information shared in the group.

Youth Track only: Place colored construction paper, markers and scissors on tables. Leave room for kids to work (Activity #2). Tape three large sheets of newsprint onto the wall side by side. Label one "My Self-Image" (Activity #2), another "God's Image of Me" (Activity #3) and the last "What I Can Do to Build My Self-Esteem" (Activity #3).

Parent Track only: Make a photocopy of the table of contents for each parent (Activity #1).

SESSION ACTIVITIES

Youth Track

1. Opening—Explain that this is a special study on "drugs, God and me." This study emphasizes that young people can live healthy Christian lives and avoid drug

Parent Track

1. Opening—Explain that this is a special study on "drugs, God and me." This study emphasizes that parents can help their junior highers live healthy Chris-

Youth Track

abuse. Encourage kids to be ready with their questions and open to new information. Explain that after each session there'll be an opportunity to meet with their parents to discuss what they've learned.

Parent Track

tian lives.

Hand out photocopies of the table of contents and briefly explain what this course covers. Talk about the three different tracks, explaining how to use the "At-Home Track" after each session. Encourage parents to rely on one another and you for support during this study.

Remind participants that since everyone will be encouraged to talk about personal information it's important to maintain a safe environment for sharing. Say: "God values each person, and that valuing can influence the way we treat one another. When we show we care for others, it helps all of us feel good. One way to care for one another is to agree on guidelines to use during our sessions." Read aloud the "Guidelines for Caring" and add other guidelines parents or junior highers feel are important.

2. Descriptive words— Hand out paper and pencils and ask young people to think about how they see themselves. Say: "If you could choose only one word to describe yourself, what would it be? Write that word on your paper. Try to use a descriptive word such as 'loved,' 'happy' or 'energetic.'

"Now think how you can write that word to display the feeling it represents. For example, you might write 'loved' in a heart. Or you might show 'energetic' by writing each letter as a moving figure. Be creative.

"After you decide on a word

2. Getting acquainted— Ask parents to form small groups of four with individuals they know the least. Have each parent share the following information: name; names and ages of children; why he or she came to this session; and what he or she hopes to learn. After parents talk within the small groups, ask each parent to pick a partner within the small group and introduce that partner to the total group. After this brief introduction, remind parents they'll have numerous opportunities to get to know one another better during the course.

Youth Track

and how to display it, go to the table and select the colored construction paper that best represents your feeling and transfer your idea to that paper."

Give kids 10 minutes to complete their words. Then ask them each to tape their words onto the newsprint labeled "My Self-Image" and explain why they chose that word.

3. What does the Bible say?—Read aloud Psalm 139:1-5, 13-18. After reading this passage, ask group members, "What does this Bible passage say to you about your creation?"

Then say, "Let's list ideas like 'I am known' and 'God understands my thoughts' that summarize God's image of you through these Bible verses." Write responses on the newsprint labeled "God's Image of Me."

Give each person a photocopy of the "A Look at Myself Through God's Eyes" handout. Read aloud the instructions and ask kids to complete Section One.

After five minutes read aloud the statements in Section One of the handout and talk about the following correct responses:

Parent Track

3. Yesterday and today—Explain that the purpose of this activity is to help parents understand what it's like to be a young person in today's world. Ask parents to remain in small groups. Say: "Being a young person in today's world isn't easy. But it wasn't always easy in the past either." Give each small group newsprint and a marker and ask the parents to brainstorm about what it was like when they were in junior high and high school. Ask groups to record their answers to the following questions:

- What kind of clothes did you wear?
- What music did you listen to?
- What did you do for fun?
- What was the "in" thing to do?
- Who were your heroes?

Youth Track

1. A, C, D
2. B, E
3. A, C
4. A, B, C, D
5. A, B, C, D

After a brief discussion, ask kids to complete Section Two of the handout. Have junior highers meet in small groups of four to list specific things they can do to develop a positive self-image. Give each group a marker and sheet of newsprint. Have a volunteer in each group list ideas, combining those that are similar. After five minutes ask small groups to share their ideas. Write these on the newsprint labeled "What I Can Do to Build My Self-Esteem."

After making the list, ask, "How can abusing drugs harm a person's self-image and self-esteem?"

Parent Track

- What were some of your generation's values?
- What were some of your generation's no-nos?
- What were some of your generation's teenage troubles?
- What was important to you as a teenager?

Give groups 20 minutes to complete this activity. Then ask groups to tape their lists onto the wall. Have each group select a spokesperson to briefly summarize the list. Ask the whole group to brainstorm for their teenagers, answering the same questions as their teenagers would. Record responses on newsprint and tape them next to the other responses. Conclude this activity by summarizing the lists. Emphasize similarities and note differences between generations.

Say: "As a parent, you have an important role in helping your young person avoid drug abuse. Your attitudes, beliefs, lifestyle and relationships within the family have a profound effect on your kids. Many people believe that preventing drug abuse begins with knowing about drugs and what they do—and that *is* part of prevention. But we're going to begin by helping young people build self-esteem.

"All of us know the way we feel about ourselves affects how

Youth Track

Parent Track

we treat our bodies. Therefore, when we help our young people develop a positive self-image, we also help them avoid drug abuse. We mentioned a few struggles young people face today. Let's briefly summarize the challenges our junior highers face, including peer pressure, physical change and drug abuse.'' Write these challenges on a sheet of newsprint so parents can see the magnitude of the struggles their kids face.

Give each parent a pencil and photocopy of the ''What Role Do I Play?'' handout. Say: ''All of us play a role in helping our young people develop positive self-esteem. Read the questions on your handout and write a response to each one.''

4. Body outlines—Say: ''Our bodies are part of who we are. When we're happy, we bounce when we walk and our eyes sparkle. When we're unhappy, our bodies show little energy and reflect the sadness inside. Being aware of ourselves means being aware of our bodies.

''When I give a signal, find a partner you feel comfortable with. I'll give each person a large sheet of newsprint and a marker. One person will lie on his or her sheet of newsprint while the

4. You're special—Ask a volunteer to read aloud Psalm 139:1-5, 13-18. Then read aloud the ''Self-esteem booster'' for this session. Give parents each a piece of paper. Ask parents to list ways they're special, not for what they *do*, but for who they *are*. For example, a parent might say, ''I'm patient and willing to listen to others before I open my mouth.'' After a few minutes have each parent select a partner. Partners should talk to each other about how they're special.

Youth Track

partner traces his or her body outline. Then switch. Write your name at the top of your body outline and tape it onto the wall. Inside your body outline, write one thing about yourself you feel good about such as 'I have naturally curly hair.' "

When everyone finishes, have group members write on every person's body outline something they like about that person. Encourage them to be specific. For example, "I like your smile" or "I like the way you laugh when you hear a funny joke." Remind kids to give positive messages since the purpose of this activity is to increase self-esteem and to help build a positive self-image.

5. Closing—After everyone has written on the others' body outlines, ask all participants to form a circle. Read aloud the "Self-esteem booster" to the group. Then ask group members

Parent Track

After partners talk, have them turn their papers over to list ways their junior highers are special. For example, a parent might say, "I appreciate my child's sensitivity to others." After a few minutes have each parent talk with the partner about ways his or her junior higher is special, not for what he or she *does*, but for who he or she *is*.

Give parents another piece of paper and have them write letters to their junior highers starting, "You're special because . . ." Explain that the letters should affirm their young people. Say: "Affirmations are positive statements we use to build a good self-image. We offer affirmations—these wonderful gifts to ourselves and our children—to express unconditional acceptance. Try not to base your affirmations on behavior since kids can interpret affirming only good behavior as conditional acceptance." Let parents know they'll share these letters with their kids during the "At-Home Track 1."

5. Closing—Ask parents to form a circle. Say: "All of you are special because God created you. There's no one else like any one of you! This is also true for your children. Help your young

Youth Track

each to say one thing about themselves for which they're thankful. Ask junior highers to begin with the statement, "I'm thankful to God that I'm . . ." After everyone has completed the statement, conclude the session with the following prayer:

"God, thank you for creating us as unique beings. Help us recognize our value in your eyes. As we celebrate our positive qualities, support us in our struggles with temptation. Encourage us to remember who we are. In our Creator's name we pray, amen."

Remind group members to take their body outlines home to share during the "At-Home Track 1" before the next session.

Parent Track

people celebrate their unique qualities, and love them as they are, not as what you think they should be.

"The junior high years aren't easy. You may find that you're questioning yourself more than ever before. You may be afraid of numerous threats to your child, including drug abuse. When these fears disturb you, remember the value of this lesson. For when your children feel good about themselves, they find it much easier to deal with the struggles common to their age group." Close the session with prayer.

Distribute photocopies of the "At-Home Track 1" handout. Explain that this handout should be completed by each junior higher and his or her parent before the next session. Encourage kids or parents to schedule a time for this at-home meeting as soon as possible.

FOR SESSION 1

Youth Track—Activity 3 Handout

A Look at Myself Through God's Eyes

Instructions: Complete each section of the handout when you're instructed to do so. Don't work ahead.

Section One. **Make a choice.** Read each of the following statements and circle *all* responses that are true.

1. God's unconditional love means:
- A. I can do nothing to stop God from loving me.
- B. God loves me only when I please him.
- C. God wants me to feel good about myself.
- D. God wants me to take good care of myself physically, emotionally and spiritually.
- E. God's only concerned about my spiritual growth.

2. To develop positive self-esteem, I'll:
- A. keep a happy face, no matter what happens.
- B. work hard to develop a good self-concept.
- C. reject all forms of drugs.
- D. rely totally on God to keep me positive and happy.
- E. take care of my physical, emotional and spiritual self.

3. Self-esteem is:
- A. a skill I can develop.
- B. something I was born with.
- C. the value I place on myself.
- D. always with me once I've experienced it.

4. Building self-esteem includes:
- A. taking risks.
- B. forgiving myself and others.
- C. developing my skills and talents.
- D. accepting compliments.

5. Drug abuse can damage:
- A. my self-image.
- B. my body.
- C. my relationship with God.
- D. my relationship with my family.

Section Two. **Make a list.** (List ideas for physical, emotional and spiritual development. For example, I can take care of my body by exercising; I can list compliments I received from others; I can remind myself I'm a special person created by God who loves me.) Ten specific things I can do to build my self-esteem:

1.	**6.**
2.	**7.**
3.	**8.**
4.	**9.**
5.	**10.**

Parent Track—Activity 3 Handout

What Role Do I Play?

Instructions: Answer all questions with specific examples.

1. What did my parents do that helped me feel valuable or important as a child?

2. What did my parents do that lowered my self-esteem or made me feel less valuable as a child?

3. Loving others begins with loving myself. How does my current self-image affect my young person?

4. How does God's love for me influence my self-image?

5. How do I convey God's unconditional love and acceptance to my young person? (Unconditional love means I am loved for who I am, not what I do.)

6. How might conditional love and acceptance harm my young person? (Conditional love means I must do something to earn love or acceptance.)

7. What am I doing to help my junior higher feel valuable?

8. What can I do to increase my child's self-esteem?

9. How can the church help my young person feel valuable?

10. In what specific ways can I help my young person build a positive self-image and enhance his or her self-esteem as a way to help prevent drug abuse?

Instructions: The "At-Home Track 1" offers junior highers and parents an opportunity to discuss the issue studied in this session. Set aside 30 minutes for this meeting.

Before you begin, remember to listen as well as talk. Arguments or put-downs don't encourage conversation. Defensiveness or shouting doesn't encourage growth or change.

Now go ahead with this meeting. Follow directions and make new discoveries about yourself and other family members.

Self-esteem booster: I'm special because God created me and there's no one else like me.

Sharing time: To begin this time together,

Parent: Give the letter you wrote to your junior higher.

Junior higher: Talk about your body outline.

Bible study: Read Genesis 1:27 together. "So God created man in his own image, in the image of God he created him; male and female he created them." Answer the following questions:

1. What does this verse say to you?
2. How can you apply this verse to your life or your family?

Activity: On a piece of paper, draw the following:

Parent: a picture of a fond memory you have of your junior higher when he or she was small.

Junior higher: a picture of a fond memory you have of your parent(s) when you were young.

Explain your drawings to each other.

On the back of your drawings, write something your parent or junior higher recently said or did to boost your self-esteem.

A plan of action: Decide on one way you can build each other's self-esteem. For example, if you want to spend more time with each other, schedule 30 minutes each week when you can do something together. Close this time by saying to each other, "I think you're special because . . ." Complete the statement with something you value in the other person, not related to what he or she does, but who he or she is.

SESSION 2

How Do I Cope With Feelings?

All people, including junior highers, need to feel close to others, understood, important and cared for. When individuals share the deepest parts of themselves and receive acceptance, they feel alive, worthwhile and secure and don't need to use drugs to deal with their feelings. Talking about thoughts and feelings with trusted friends can relieve pain and spread joy, but this kind of intimate sharing isn't always easy. This session helps parents and junior highers develop communication and support relationships within families and with other people.

This session builds on the self-esteem discussion in Session 1. For people to communicate they must look at who they really are. This is difficult for junior highers who are only beginning to know who they are apart from their parents. These young people are forced to evaluate what they're willing to reveal and what they feel they must hide. Reaching beyond themselves to communicate their feelings is much easier when they love and accept themselves. The well-known commandment to "Love your neighbor as yourself" (Matthew 19:19b) demands self-love before reaching out to communicate love to others.

OBJECTIVES

In this session junior highers and parents will:

- learn about the importance of expressing feelings.
- discuss ways to deal with feelings.
- discuss communication (expressing feelings) as an alternative to drug abuse.

SUPPLIES

- ☐ newsprint
- ☐ markers
- ☐ small strips of paper
- ☐ pads of paper
- ☐ pencils
- ☐ basket
- ☐ masking tape
- ☐ Bibles

"Youth Track" only

- ☐ paper cups
- ☐ punch

PREPARATION

Read the session and photocopy the handouts.

Before the meeting, write the following "Self-esteem booster" on newsprint and tape it onto the wall: "God understands my feelings and helps me cope with them."

Youth Track only: On a sheet of newsprint taped to the wall, copy this drawing for Activity #4.

Barriers to Expressing Feelings

Parent Track only: On newsprint, copy the following "Ways Junior Highers Deal With Their Feelings." Tape it onto the wall when indicated in Activity #6.

Ways Junior Highers Deal With Their Feelings

Healthy	Unhealthy
Become aware of feelings.	Keep them hidden.
Acknowledge and accept feelings.	Blame others.
Find healthy ways of expressing feelings.	Blow up.
	Take drugs.

SESSION ACTIVITIES

1. Opening—Respond to participants' questions or comments about the last session or the "At-Home Track 1" handout.

Youth Track

2. Feelings—Ask kids to think about feelings they've experienced recently. Some may have felt hopeful, excited or confused. Others may have felt bored, embarrassed or irritated. Give a pencil and small strip of paper to each person. Have individuals each write one feeling on a strip of paper. When everyone finishes writing, collect the papers in a basket. Ask kids to form groups of four while you sort the papers and eliminate duplicate feelings.

If kids have trouble thinking of feelings, suggest some of the following: afraid, angry, ashamed, caring, confident, daring, determined, envious, frustrated, guilty, impatient, lonely, playful, relieved, stressed, surprised.

Parent Track

2. Feelings—Hand out pencils and strips of paper. Have parents each think of one feeling they tried to communicate to their young person this week and write it on a strip of paper. Collect the papers in a basket. Ask the parents to form groups of four while you sort the papers and eliminate duplicate feelings.

Give each small group a pad of paper. Say: "Select one person from your group to meet me in the center of the room. I'll select a paper from the basket and quietly read it to them. Then these people will return to their groups and wait for a signal to begin. Without speaking, these people will draw pictures to help their group guess what the feeling is. When your group correctly identifies the feeling, raise your hands." If participants have difficulty identifying the feeling, instruct the artist to give one-word verbal clues. Repeat the activity until all feelings have been identified and written on a sheet of newsprint taped to the wall.

Youth Track

When everyone guesses the feeling written on the strips of paper, have kids look at the list. Ask: "How does your body react when you experience these feelings? Is your stomach tight? Does your head hurt? Do you feel dizzy or wound up? Pick a feeling and tell us how your body reacts."

3. How do I feel?—After briefly discussing several feelings, give each person a photocopy of the "How Do I Feel?" handout. Have kids follow instructions.

Parent Track

When parents have identified the feelings listed on the strips of paper, say: "Sometimes it's difficult to deal with feelings, our own and those of our young people. We don't know what to say or do to let our children know how we feel about them. We're also confused about how to respond to their feelings, many times because we're not sure what their feelings are. This uncertainty affects all communication in the home."

3. Communication levels—Give each parent a photocopy of the "Communication Levels" handout. Say: "The five basic communication levels described by John Powell in his book *Why Am I Afraid to Tell You Who I Am?* (Tabor Publishing) range from superficial exchanges to deeply meaningful conversations. These five levels illustrate how productive conversations can promote closeness and encourage personal growth.

"Let's read together the information and examples for each communication level. Then you can individually write an example of each communication level as it occurred in your home. Think about your own conversations or those of your young people."

Youth Track

Parent Track

Read the information together and answer any questions parents might have. Allow parents time to complete the handout on their own.

When parents complete their handouts, ask volunteers to read the example they wrote for each level. Clarify misunderstandings and offer additional guidance.

Then say: "Young people who relate to others on these last three communication levels are less likely to develop an unhealthy relationship with drugs. When young people can talk about their ideas and feelings and experience empathy from the important people in their lives, these communication skills help them develop interpersonal support and growth. With this deeper kind of communication, young people begin to understand who they are, what they believe and how they can react emotionally. They develop confidence in their personal identity and worth." Remind parents to keep the "Communication Levels" handout for the "At-Home Track 2" this week.

4. Breaking barriers—When everyone completes the handout, have kids form five groups to discuss one of the situations. After five minutes, ask

4. Role plays—Have parents form small groups of three to practice communication. Ask parents within each small group to assume the role of parent,

Youth Track

the following questions about each situation:

• What were some common feelings in your group?

• What feelings were different from most people's in the group?

• What were some common body reactions?

• What body reactions were different from most people's in the group?

Say: "The situations on this handout are typical experiences for young people. Sometimes you find it easy to talk about your feelings, but other times it's almost impossible." (Junior highers' feelings can be inhibited by a variety of fears that turn into defensive barriers. If these fears aren't faced, they can block healthy communication and prevent intimacy. Normally the feelings behind these fears won't disappear but will be expressed in other ways, some unhealthy and destructive.) "Let's list barriers to expressing feelings. One example might be that you're afraid of what other people might think. What are other fears or barriers that might block expressing feelings?" List these on the newsprint labeled "Barriers to Expressing Feelings." Examples of barriers:

Parent Track

junior higher or observer. Inform the "parent" that he or she has three distinct responsibilities as a good listener:

• The parent must acknowledge that he or she heard the junior higher by feeding back the feelings and content the junior higher expressed.

• The parent must indicate respect for the junior higher's interpretation of the situation and his or her feelings.

• The parent must use "I statements" to express his or her thoughts or feelings like "I understood you to say that you weren't sure anyone else could understand your feelings."

The "junior higher" in each small group initiates the conversation and reacts the way a kid would normally react. Encourage parents to use their own junior higher's reactions and responses in the role plays.

The "observer" in each small group listens to the words and observes what happens in the role play. The observer reports what he or she sees and hears to the other two when the role play is over.

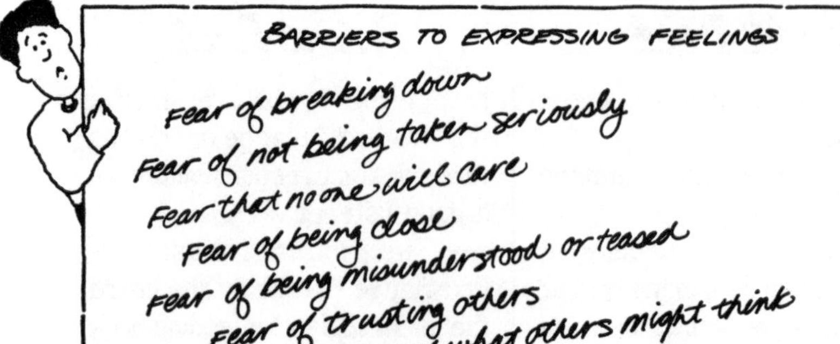

Youth Track

Say: "Most people, including parents, experience fears or barriers to expressing feelings. And you hear all kinds of advice on how to handle your feelings. Your teachers have probably given you numerous tools to overcome these fears and opportunities to use them. Your parents have probably reassured you that they'll be there whenever you need them. Your friends have probably declared their loyalty and provide encouragement when you struggle.

"You also may have heard arguments that drugs can help you cope with your feelings. Some of you may have watched friends or family members use drugs to cope. Some of your friends or acquaintances may have urged you to use drugs. Choose a partner and tell each other arguments people use to get others to try drugs to cope with their feelings.

Parent Track

Read the following "Situations" one at a time. Ask parents to switch roles each time you read a new situation. This way every parent can play each role.

Situations

Situation 1: Your son, age 12, brings home a note from his teacher saying that he was in a fight with another boy.

Situation 2: Your daughter, age 13, was offered a marijuana joint by her best friend.

Situation 3: Your son, age 14, has a bad case of acne. Today he says he's too ill to go to school, but you see no signs of illness.

When parents discuss all three situations, ask for questions or concerns about how to be a good listener.

Youth Track

For example, drugs help you feel relaxed around friends."

5. Drugs won't work—Give each pair a sheet of newsprint and marker. After a few minutes ask each pair to present the arguments for using drugs and write them on newsprint. After partners list several arguments ask every two pairs to meet together, and assign each group of four an argument. Give each small group a new sheet of newsprint. Ask group members to list as many reasons as they can why drugs won't work, according to their argument. After a few minutes have each small group tape its list onto the wall and talk about the reasons presented.

After listening to the reasons drugs won't help us express feelings, say: "Sometimes we may be unsure how to respond to individuals trying to help us deal with our feelings. The Bible offers several suggestions." Have different volunteers read aloud to the group each of the following scripture passages: Psalm 4:4; Ephesians 4:26, 31-32; and Colossians 3:12-14. Then ask: "What did you learn from these passages about how to handle feelings? What other ideas can you offer about how to handle

Parent Track

5. My personal concerns—Give each parent a photocopy of the "My Personal Concerns" handout. Read the instructions together. Ask parents to complete the handout alone.

When parents complete their responses, ask them to return to their small groups of three and talk about the handout. Remind parents this is the time to deal with their personal concerns. When parents have talked, encourage them to help and reassure one another.

Youth Track

feelings?" List ideas on a sheet of newsprint taped to the wall. Use the following ideas to enhance the list.

Unhealthy ways junior highers deal with their feelings are:

• **Keep them hidden.** Sometimes young people hide their feelings or pretend they aren't there by denying or ignoring them. Some may even try to convince themselves that they don't have any feelings. Individuals who do this sometimes get stomachaches or headaches from keeping their feelings inside. When a young person begins to have chronic stomachaches or headaches, particularly in stressful situations, that person should ask himself or herself: "What am I feeling? Why?"

• **Blame others.** Young people do this to avoid responsibility for their feelings. When they believe someone else causes their feelings, they erroneously think that person can make them feel better. So they look to others to improve their feelings rather than deal with feelings on their own.

• **Blow up.** Physical and emotional developmental changes cause young people to hold their feelings inside for long periods of time. Uncertain of what's normal or acceptable, young people bury

Parent Track

Youth Track

their feelings and then explode at unexpected times. Pressures build until young people can no longer contain them. When this happens, the rational mind loses control. Individuals do or say things they later regret. Extreme forms of this reaction result in physical or emotional abuse of others.

• **Take drugs.** Some young people use drugs to temporarily relieve internal stress that results from unexpressed emotions. Marijuana and alcohol are among the drugs kids most commonly use. When kids can reduce their physical stress and relieve the guilt associated with suppressed feelings, they feel better. But relief is temporary. When the drug wears off, old feelings remain and still need to be dealt with.

Healthy ways junior highers deal with their feelings are:

• **Become aware of feelings.** With all the new and different feelings that are part of their physical and emotional development, junior highers may not know they're having certain feelings until these feelings suddenly erupt.

• **Acknowledge and accept feelings.** When junior highers learn that feelings aren't "good" or "bad" they can acknowledge

Parent Track

Youth Track

and accept those feelings and express them to others.

• **Find healthy ways of expressing feelings.** With all the changes and emotional upheavals during the junior high years, it's important for young people to find healthy ways to deal with their feelings. Physical activity, hobbies or other opportunities for self-expression help kids learn when and where to release their emotional energy. Sports and music provide natural opportunities for venting feelings.

6. Alone time—Have junior highers look at the feelings in the first activity. Say: "We've talked about the feelings you have around others. Now it's important to get in touch with the feelings you have when you're alone. When I give the signal, move around the room and find a place you can be alone and comfortable. Some of you may lie on the floor. Others may feel more comfortable in a chair. Make sure you're far enough apart that you don't disturb others and they don't disturb you."

Give a signal for everyone to move. After everyone finds his or her place to be alone, encourage participants to get comfortable. Ask participants to shut

Parent Track

6. Communication tips—While parents meet, tape onto the wall the newsprint you prepared with healthy and unhealthy "Ways Junior Highers Deal With Their Feelings."

Remind parents they're not alone. Read aloud Psalm 139:7-10. Say: "It's important to know you aren't alone when you try to talk with your child about feelings. God is with you and he willingly supports you as you try to communicate with your young person.

"Look at the list of healthy and unhealthy ways junior highers deal with their feelings. How can you help your child when he or she struggles with feelings?"

After a brief discussion, say: "Communication plays a vital

Youth Track

their eyes and remain quiet. After 30 seconds, say: "Get in touch with what you're feeling right now. What's your body saying to you? How does your stomach feel? your head? your feet and hands? your muscles? What's your breathing like?"

"Are you relaxed or tense? Do you feel like moving around or sleeping? Is one particular part of your body demanding more attention than others? Listen to your body messages." (Pause 10 seconds.)

"What's your body telling you about how you feel? Are your arms and legs stiff or relaxed? Is your mind able to let things go or is it struggling to stay in control of this situation?" (Pause 10 seconds.)

"Think about why you're feeling the way you are. Were you aware of these feelings prior to this activity?" (Pause 10 seconds.)

"Do you need to talk about your feelings with someone? Think of who you'd like to talk to. What would you say to that person?" (Pause 10 seconds.)

"How would you like to respond to the feelings you're having now? Do you feel a need to do something or are you content to experience what's happening?" (Pause 10 seconds.)

Parent Track

role in helping kids discover how to deal with their feelings. Talk about clear communication and use these suggestions when you and your kids talk with one another." Read aloud the following points:

• Listen with an open mind. Be careful not to judge each other until each of you listens to what the other has to say. Only when an individual understands the motivation for another's actions can he or she understand that person's behavior.

By listening to young people and encouraging their creativity, parents support positive opportunities for venting feelings.

• Remember that feelings aren't right or wrong, good or bad. Emotional responses indicate that individuals are struggling with thoughts they've had or situations in which they were involved. The feeling itself isn't wrong or bad; however, the way the feeling is expressed can be healthy or unhealthy.

Parents can help young people recognize feelings by reporting what's taken place. For example, if a young person explodes like a volcano to a parent's request to pick up a jacket, the parent can calmly respond: "When I asked you to pick up your jacket, you screamed at me and told

Youth Track

When everyone settles down, say: "Now that you're in touch with your body and feelings, I'd like each of you to take a special journey. Relax. Keep your eyes closed. Listen to your heart beat and the rhythm of your breathing. Tell your nerves and muscles to relax from your toes up. Try to let go of all thoughts and relax your mind.

"Think of a place you like to be alone, that's quiet and peaceful. Picture this place in your mind. Some of you may have a quiet place at home—your room, an attic or by a tree in your yard. Others may have a special place somewhere else—a table in the school library, a rock near a lake or the chapel at church. Think about your quiet place and imagine yourself there.

"Now imagine God is with you. Invite him to sit beside you and show him all the things that make this place special to you. Smell the familiar smells. Listen to familiar sounds. Feel the warmth or coolness of the air. Talk to God about how you feel when you're here.

"Thank God for visiting you in your quiet place. Let him know how much you appreciate his being there to listen and understand how you feel. Thank God for caring about you, being your friend

Parent Track

me to leave you alone. I'm concerned about why this request made you so angry."

Parents can guide their young people in expressing feelings without abusing others. Because feelings are difficult to deal with when young people express them, parents may wait for feelings to subside before they talk with their young person about what happened. When the junior higher understands what he or she said or did, the parent can initiate talking about why. Expressing concern about a young person's emotional outburst is much more effective than screaming at the kid not to do it again.

Parents can acknowledge that it's hard for their kids to accept other people telling them what to do when they're trying to become independent and think for themselves, but it's important for junior highers to consider others' feelings. For example, the parent might say: "If you'd told me you were planning to wear that jacket and you were late for your paper route, I would've felt much better. You were under stress, but a quick explanation could've helped my feelings and I might've helped you with your paper route."

• Integrate feelings into the

Youth Track

and sharing your special place. When you're ready to leave your quiet place, ask God to be with you as you come back to the room we're in.

"Open your eyes and meet with four other people near you." Read aloud each of the following questions and ask the groups to discuss them:

• What was it like to get in touch with your feelings? Did it come naturally or was it hard to concentrate? Why?

• Were you aware of your feelings prior to this activity?

• Did you decide to talk to someone about your feelings? Why or why not?

• What did you learn about yourself from this activity?

Give each person a copy of the "How I Can Cope With My Feelings" handout. Say: "Sometimes when we're stressed, it's hard to remember how to cope with your feelings. Read the suggestions on this handout and think about ways you can use each suggestion. Keep this paper and discuss it with your parent in the 'At-Home Track 2' meeting this week."

Parent Track

"whole" person. When a young person experiencing a feeling can acknowledge it, think about why the feeling is present and decide whether to express it, he or she has developed self-control. You can help your young people recognize and work with their feelings rather than allow emotions to control them.

• Acknowledge that feelings don't disappear. If kids don't express feelings, they'll find some other way to release them. For example, a person hurt by a friend's action may avoid the friend until that person talks about the pain. Talking about feelings is one way young people can understand themselves better. They may begin to notice patterns or repetition of certain emotional responses and work on them. For example, if young people are often angry and disappointed by friends, they may realize that their previously hidden expectations for friends are too high. Examining and lowering expectations may result in less anger.

Say: "These suggestions for clear communication can help you and your young person get to know each other better. They can initiate conversation about feelings and open channels of communication about tough is-

Youth Track

7. Closing—Ask group members to form a circle. Have a volunteer read the "Self-esteem booster." Give each person a paper cup and marker. Say: "On the bottom of your cup, write an affirmation for the person on your right. Then fill the cup with punch from the refreshment table and give it to the person."

When everyone receives the cup of punch, close with the following prayer: "God, thank you for giving us feelings. Thank you for understanding our feelings even when we don't understand them ourselves. Help us cope with our feelings in ways that please you. In Jesus' name, amen."

Parent Track

sues such as drug abuse."

7. Closing—Give each parent a photocopy of the "How Am I Doing?" handout. Say: "Spend the next few minutes looking at yourself. Respond to each item. Circle those responses you want to work on during the week."

After five minutes, say: "This self-evaluation gives each of you a look at what you do right and uncovers areas you may want to work on. Talk with a close friend or spouse about those things you need to improve. Ask your junior higher to talk about areas in which he or she can use your help. Talk with God about your feelings and ask for help."

Ask parents to form a circle. Read aloud the "Self-esteem booster" for this session. Say: "Let's close by thanking God for one specific feeling he's helped you understand and cope with. Talk to God now about that feeling and how he's helped you grow." After a minute of silence, offer the following prayer: "God, thank you for your presence and understanding with each of us. Help us be as understanding with our own children as you are with us. Use us as role models to help our young people grow into the adults you want them to be. In the name of our perfect role

Youth Track	Parent Track
	model, Jesus Christ, we pray, amen."

Distribute photocopies of the "At-Home Track 2" handout. Explain that this handout should be completed by each junior higher and his or her parent before the next session. Encourage kids or parents to schedule a time for this at-home meeting as soon as possible.

FOR SESSION 2

Youth Track—Activity 3 Handout

How Do I Feel?

Instructions: In the "Feeling" column, draw the feelings you might have in each situation. In the "Body reaction" column, describe how your body might react to each situation.

Situation	**Feeling**	**Body reaction**
Example:		
A friend moves away.	 	tears, no energy, a lump in my throat, headache

 You flunk your math test.

 Your parent says he or she is proud of you.

 Your dog is critically injured by a car.

 You hear strange noises when you're home alone.

 A new friend calls and asks you to spend the night.

Parent Track—Activity 3 Handout

Communication Levels

Instructions: Read about each communication level. Write at least one example of this communication level in your home.

1. Clichés. (This is the most superficial communication level. Conversational clichés are the polite greetings and standard statements people use to begin and end conversations.)

Examples: "Hello, how are you?"
"Nice weather, isn't it?"
"Have a good day!"

Example from home:

2. Facts. (No personal revelations occur. The speaker is merely an objective reporter.)

Examples: "Did you hear that the president has a cancerous tumor?"
"Let me tell you about Bill."
"This newspaper article says the woman was charged with the crime."

Example from home:

3. Ideas and judgments. (This kind of communication is more personal and reveals how a person thinks. It can sometimes initiate more intimate conversation. When people tell others what they think, they often look at others' reactions to see if these people agree and how they judge their views.)

Examples: "I don't think my music teacher likes me."
"I'm sure this person is the best candidate for the job."
"It'd be great if we had more free time between classes."

Example from home:

4. Feelings. (If people respect what someone thinks, they're more likely to seek this communication level. When individuals communicate feelings, they risk letting people know who they are. But this kind of conversation is more than a risk. It's also an opportunity to break down barriers and get closer to the other person. It's a chance to reveal inner emotions and feelings that make an individual different from someone else.)

Examples: "I'm nervous about going to the spring formal with David."
"I really hope I earned a position in the starting lineup."
"I'm afraid to ask my parents for money."

Example from home:

5. Mutual sharing. (This is the deepest communication level. This experience usually occurs between close friends, brothers and sisters or other family members and is called empathy.)

Example: Individuals feel each other's joy and pain. They may cry together or celebrate each other's victories.

Example from home:

Instructions: Write your personal response to each concern. Be prepared to talk about your responses in your small group.

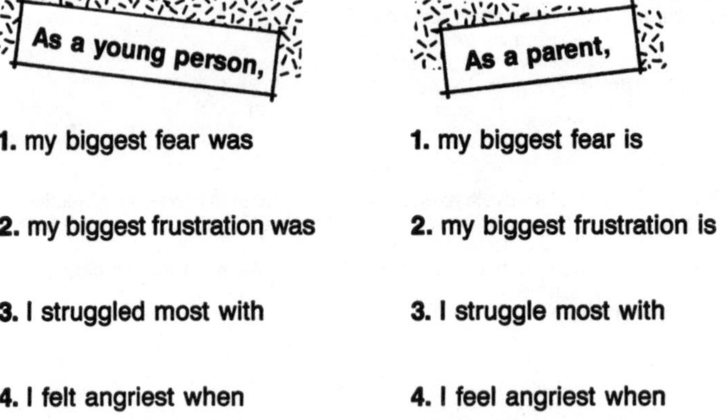

As a young person,

1. my biggest fear was
2. my biggest frustration was
3. I struggled most with
4. I felt angriest when
5. what I wanted most was

As a parent,

1. my biggest fear is
2. my biggest frustration is
3. I struggle most with
4. I feel angriest when
5. my greatest dream for my child is

If I were a junior higher today, I would struggle most with

When it comes to talking with my child about drug abuse, I generally feel

Youth Track—Activity 6 Handout

How I Can Cope With My Feelings

Instructions: Read each of the following suggestions and list specific ways you use each of these ideas in your life.

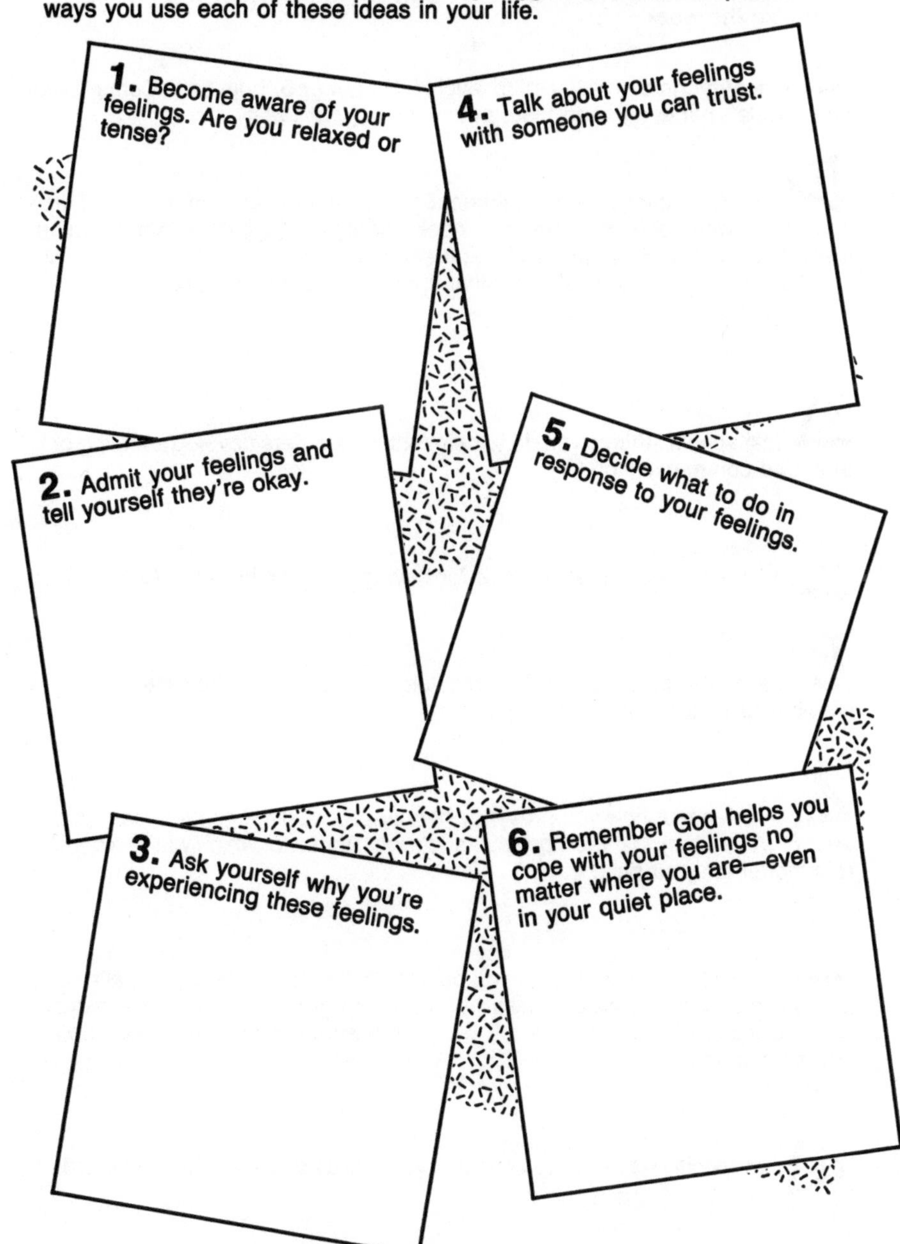

Parent Track—Activity 7 Handout

How Am I Doing?

Instructions: Respond to each item. Circle those items you want to work on during the week.

1. Identify the communication level (1, 2, 3, 4 or 5, from the "Communication Levels" handout) used most frequently in your family.

2. List the names of your children. Estimate the amount of individual time you spend with each child during a week. Identify the typical communication level (1, 2, 3, 4 or 5) between you and each child.

Name	Minutes of individual time	Communication level

3. List specific things you do to help family members develop a feeling of trust and communication.

4. List activities you encourage for having fun together as a family.

5. Identify individuals (inside and outside the family) to whom each family member turns for emotional support.

6. Think about how you presently handle your feelings (anger, fear, sadness or frustration). List feelings you handle well, those for which you're a good role model for your child.

7. List drugs and chemicals you personally use. (Include aspirin, allergy medication, cough syrups and nasal sprays, along with alcohol and other more potent drugs. Rate yourself as a role model in this area: bad, poor, okay, good or outstanding.)

8. List specific ways you've educated your child about drugs and their use.

Instructions: The "At-Home Track 2" offers junior highers and parents an opportunity to discuss the issue studied in this session. Set aside 30 minutes for this meeting.

Before you begin, remember to listen as well as talk. Arguments or put-downs don't encourage conversation. Defensiveness or shouting doesn't encourage growth or change.

Now go ahead with this meeting. Follow directions and make new discoveries about yourself and other family members.

Self-esteem booster: God understands my feelings and helps me cope with them.

Sharing time: To begin this time together,

Parent: Briefly explain the five "Communication Levels" to your junior higher.

Junior higher: Talk with your parent about the ideas on the "How I Can Cope With My Feelings" handout.

Bible study: Read Ephesians 6:1-4 together. "Children, obey your parents in the Lord, for this is right. 'Honor your father and mother'—which is the first commandment with a promise—'that it may go well with you and that you may enjoy long life on the earth.' Fathers, do not exasperate your children; instead, bring them up in the training and instruction of the Lord." Answer the following questions:

1. What does this passage say to you?
2. How can you apply this passage to your life or your family?

Activity: Separately list five good feelings you have for other family members. Don't let anyone see your list. Using a pad of paper, take turns drawing out and guessing each other's feelings. If others can't guess your feelings, give one-word verbal clues.

List those good feelings here.

A plan of action: Use some of the following "Discussion Starters" during your meals this week. Ask each person to choose one statement he or she would like to complete.

Concentrate on keeping the communication in levels three, four or five on the "Communication Levels" handout. Use this opportunity to understand and help each other cope with feelings.

Discussion Starters

1. The happiest time of my life was . . .
2. What worries me about the future is . . .
3. It's hard to tell others what I feel inside because . . .
4. The hardest subject to discuss with my junior higher (parent) is . . .
5. One thing I do well that my junior higher (parent) doesn't know about is . . .

SESSION 3

Taking a Look at Drugs

After helping young people develop positive self-esteem and opening communication channels to talk more deeply, parents can concentrate on learning about drugs. They can learn how to help their junior highers make positive choices about using chemicals properly or avoiding them completely.

Too often adults have inaccurate or incomplete information about drugs. When they use false or incomplete information to talk with their young people about their concerns, they soon lose credibility with their kids. Before parents can make a wise choice or talk with kids about choices, parents need to have accurate information about the drugs most available to young people today. Knowledge of the drugs, their legitimate uses and their dangers will provide a foundation for the rest of this prevention program.

OBJECTIVES

In this session junior highers and parents will:

- educate themselves about drugs.
- talk about drug-related terms.
- learn about psychoactive drugs and how they affect the body.
- discuss reasons for drug use.
- discuss alternatives to drug use.
- examine media messages about drugs.

SUPPLIES

- ☐ newsprint
- ☐ markers
- ☐ pencils
- ☐ masking tape
- ☐ Bible

"Parent Track" only

- ☐ paper

"Youth Track" only

- ☐ magazines
- ☐ glue
- ☐ scissors
- ☐ large sheets of construction paper
- ☐ 3×5 cards

PREPARATION

Read the session and photocopy the handouts.

Before the meeting, write the following "Self-esteem booster" on newsprint and tape it onto the wall: "I'm a caretaker of God's creations. I must use his creations wisely."

Write "Drugs" on newsprint and tape it onto the wall (Activity #1).

Youth Track only: Tape a sheet of newsprint onto the wall. Label it "Why Do People Use Drugs?" (Activity #3).

Set up a large table (Activity #2).

Parent Track only: Tape a sheet of newsprint onto the wall. Label it "Alternatives to Drugs" (Activity #4).

SESSION ACTIVITIES

1. Opening—Respond to participants' questions or comments about the last session or the "At-Home Track 2" handout.

Then ask, "How would you define drugs?" Write responses on the newsprint labeled "Drugs." Allow several people to offer their input. If no one says anything about over-the-counter medications or drugs found in cigarettes, foods or drinks, ask, "What about . . .?" You'll find out right away how much parents and young people know, or don't know, about drugs.

Youth Track

2. Crossword puzzle—Ask group members to form teams of four. Give each team a pencil, photocopy of the "What Do You Know About Drugs?" crossword puzzle and photocopy of the "Drug Information" handout. Say: "You have 15 minutes to complete 'What Do You Know About Drugs?' You can find all the answers in the 'Drug Information' handout."

When time is up or groups complete their puzzles, read aloud each crossword puzzle clue and answer and have kids correct their answers. This introduction and immediate reinforcement helps them remember terms used throughout the rest of the sessions.

Answers for the "What Do You Know About Drugs?" Crossword Puzzle.

Across	**Down**
2. psychoactive	1. inhalants
4. abstinence	3. amphetamines
8. intoxication	5. blackout
9. OTC	6. controlled
11. THC	7. withdrawal
12. LSD	10. PCP
13. alcohol	14. barbiturates
15. marijuana	17. stimulants
16. trip	18. drug
18. deliriants	19. tolerance
23. dependence	20. overdose
24. cocaine	21. addiction
26. depressants	22. caffeine
27. narcotics	24. crack
28. hallucinogens	25. nicotine

Parent Track

2. Drug IQ—Give each parent a pencil and a photocopy of the "Drug IQ Quiz" handout. Say: "This quiz tests your knowledge of major points about drugs. Read the questions and circle the letter of the response you think is correct."

When parents finish their quiz, read the following answers.

1. e	3. c	5. d	7. d	9. a
2. b	4. d	6. c	8. b	10. d

Then say: "How did you do? Are you an expert? Even if you answered all these questions correctly, there's still a lot to learn about drugs."

Youth Track

Place magazines, scissors and glue on the table. Give each junior higher a pencil and large sheet of construction paper. Say: "The media sends us many messages about drugs. In this activity, we'll look at those messages and the myths that are perpetuated about drugs. Cut out three advertisements for any kind of drug use and glue them to your construction paper." Tell participants to write the answers to the following questions next to each advertisement:

- What message does this advertisement give concerning drugs?
- What false message does the advertisement give?
- What audience is this advertisement targeting? Who would respond to this ad?

Say: "For example, the message of a cigarette advertisement might be that smoking cigarettes makes a person more attractive to the opposite sex. The false message is that smoking cigarettes makes a person more attractive. The targeted audience of this ad might be young men and women."

After kids finish their papers, have individuals explain their ads and answers to the total

Parent Track

Youth Track

group. Encourage others to add observations as people talk.

3. Why drugs?—Ask: "Why do people use drugs? Why do kids at your school use drugs? What reasons do they give?" Write these responses on the newsprint labeled "Why Do People Use Drugs?"

After group members suggest at least 10 reasons for drug use, have them identify needs for each reason. For example, if kids say one reason people use drugs is to relax around friends, they might identify a need for personal self-esteem.

Have participants meet in pairs and give each pair a photocopy of the "Why Drugs?" handout. Assign each pair one reason for drug use and have them write the reason and need on their worksheet. Then ask each pair to brainstorm together about alternatives for meeting that need. For example, if a person needs to develop self-esteem, the pair might suggest encouraging that person to develop his or her talents such as playing the piano or designing a computer program. (Assigning different pairs the same reason isn't a prob-

Parent Track

3. Crossword puzzle—Give each parent a photocopy of the "What Do You Know About Drugs?" crossword puzzle and the "Drug Information" handout. Say: "Work with a partner to complete this crossword puzzle. You can find all the answers in the 'Drug Information' handout."

When time is up, ask volunteers to read each crossword puzzle clue and answer and help parents correct their answers. This introduction and immediate reinforcement helps parents remember terms used throughout the rest of the sessions. Encourage parents to take this information home to use as a resource.

Youth Track

lem since brainstorming usually provides different ideas.)

After pairs brainstorm their ideas and write them on the handout, ask each pair to read their reason people use drugs, explain what need is reflected and act out one of their alternatives for the total group. Have the rest of the group members guess what the alternative is. After group members guess correctly, ask participants to add other alternatives they think would be effective. Then have each pair tape their handout over the responses for "Why Do People Use Drugs?"

4. How does drug use affect me?—Give each person a photocopy of the "How Does Drug Use Affect Me?" handout. Ask each person to complete this handout alone. Let kids know they'll talk about only as many of their answers on this handout as they want.

Give individuals a 3×5 card and ask them to write any questions they still have about drugs. Collect cards and answer the questions that you can. Let the kids know you'll look for answers to their questions and answer them at the beginning of the next session. Have individuals sign their card

Parent Track

4. Why drugs?—Have parents form two groups. Give each group a sheet of newsprint and a marker. Ask one group to list the reasons junior highers give for using drugs. Ask the other group to list the reasons the media give for using drugs. When parents make the lists, have the two groups exchange lists and write what needs are expressed for each reason listed. For example, if the media suggest using drugs as a way to make someone attractive, the need might be a lack of self-esteem in interacting with peers of the opposite sex. Or if junior highers say

Youth Track

if they want a private answer.

Parent Track

they use drugs in order to be part of a group, the need could be fear of being alone.

When both groups have identified the needs, bring the groups together and say: "We've discovered what the media and junior highers see as kids' needs today. It's important for us to know different ways we can respond to these strong messages about what's important to kids.

"Look at the needs you've identified. Suggest activities or other alternatives that meet those needs for junior highers." List ideas on the sheet of newsprint labeled "Alternatives to Drugs."

Give parents each a sheet of paper and ask them to list their children's needs. Suggest parents look at the list of alternatives and ask themselves: "Would any of these alternatives meet my junior higher's needs? Would my junior higher accept these ideas?"

When parents identify the needs and alternatives their junior highers would accept, have parents each plan how they can help their junior higher meet one of his or her special needs this week. For example, one father might recognize his daughter's need

Youth Track

5. Closing—Ask group members to form a circle and talk about one alternative to drug use that they use. Have them explain what need they meet by using this alternative. For example, one person might say: "Sometimes I want to escape everything going on around me, so I curl up on my bed and read a book."

After each person talks about one alternative he or she uses, read aloud Genesis 1:27-31a. Say: "God created human beings to be in charge of the plants of the earth and everything else he created. We have a responsibility to use his creations wisely." Close the meeting with the following prayer: "God, we are caretakers of your creations. Help us use our

Parent Track

to feel more comfortable around boys. He could make a dinner "date" with her during the week and talk about what to expect in the dating scene. This could help her develop confidence in how to act around boys and help to initiate a special relationship with her father as well. Realizing her father cares enough to take this time with her alone can boost a young junior higher's self-esteem.

5. Closing—Ask parents to think about their actions and attitudes toward using drugs. Have them turn their paper over and list the alternatives to drug use that they model for their junior highers. Ask each parent to talk about one positive alternative he or she can model. For example, one parent may decide to limit his intake of caffeine by drinking only decaffeinated coffee after noon.

Read the "Self-esteem booster" and ask a volunteer to read Genesis 1:27-31a. Close the session with the following prayer: "God, thank you for our junior highers who force us to look at ourselves and how we model your will for our lives. Make us responsible for our choices as parents and

Youth Track

minds and bodies to glorify what you've created. Be with us as we think about drugs and how they affect our bodies. Help us make good decisions about how to use all that is part of your creation. In Jesus' name we pray, amen."

Parent Track

caretakers of your creation. Give us your loving Spirit as we talk to those we love about the dangers of drug abuse. In the name of the perfect role model, Jesus Christ, amen."

Distribute photocopies of the "At-Home Track 3" handout. Explain that this handout should be completed by each junior higher and his or her parent before the next session. Encourage kids or parents to schedule a time for this at-home meeting as soon as possible.

Parent Track—Activity 2 Handout

Drug IQ Quiz

Instructions: For each question, circle the letter of the response you think is correct.

1. Drug abuse is likely to be a problem in the following age group(s):
(a) 12-16.
(b) 17-25.
(c) 26-45.
(d) 46 and over.
(e) all of the above.

2. Most drug users make their first contact with illegal drugs:
(a) through "pushers" seeking new customers.
(b) through their friends.
(c) accidentally.
(d) all of the above.

3. The drug most commonly abused in the United States is:
(a) cocaine.
(b) marijuana.
(c) alcohol.
(d) heroin.

4. Stimulants excite the central nervous system. Which of the following drugs isn't a stimulant?
(a) cocaine.
(b) amphetamines.
(c) caffeine.
(d) barbiturates.

5. Using marijuana can affect the human body by:
(a) altering brain functions.
(b) interfering in the reproductive process.
(c) affecting the lungs.
(d) all of the above.

6. Marijuana:
(a) reduces a person's ability to see.
(b) is a stimulant.
(c) influences coordination and reaction time.
(d) all of the above.

7. Depressants:
(a) slow the body's physical and mental activities.
(b) are addictive.
(c) are more dangerous than stimulants.
(d) all of the above.

8. Hallucinogens:
(a) come only from plants.
(b) affect people differently.
(c) have no positive value.
(d) all of the above.

9. Alcohol is a:
(a) depressant.
(b) hallucinogen.
(c) narcotic.
(d) stimulant.

10. Cocaine:
(a) can be snorted, injected and smoked.
(b) is highly addictive.
(c) is a stimulant.
(d) all of the above.

Youth Track—Activity 2 Handout
Parent Track—Activity 3 Handout

Drug Information

Drug terminology. People often use the following terms when talking about drugs:

1. **Drug.** A drug is a chemical that, even in small doses, can produce significant changes in the body and mind.
   Most of us have a general idea of what a drug is. Sometimes, however, it's difficult to distinguish a drug from a food. For example, sugar strongly affects the body, but it also has nutritive value; therefore, sugar is a food. Alcohol is a food because it contains calories, yet it's also a powerful drug. Alcoholic beverages have little or no nutritive value.
2. **Tolerance.** Tolerance means the body can learn to adjust to (tolerate) the presence of a drug.
   When someone builds tolerance to a drug, that person must ingest more and more of the drug to get the desired effect.
3. **Dependence.** When someone regularly uses a drug and relies on it for performing normal activities, this individual is said to be "dependent" on the drug.
   Individuals can be psychologically dependent on a drug without being physically addicted to it. They think they must have the drug for emotional reasons such as relaxing before school, but their body doesn't physically crave the drug. When people are psychologically "dependent" on a drug, they often experience depression or nervousness when they stop using it.
4. **Addiction.** Physical dependence on a drug is addiction.
   Addiction occurs when the drug user's body adjusts to continuous drug use and must physically readjust to function without the drug. Withdrawal is physically painful; some people even die from drug withdrawal.
5. **Withdrawal.** When an addicted person stops using the drug, he or she suffers physical withdrawal symptoms. The person's mind and body must try to readjust to living without the drug.
   Physical withdrawal symptoms may vary according to the drug used. For example, withdrawal from alcohol, a drug that depresses the central nervous system (the brain and spinal cord), results in nervousness, sleep disruption, motor agitation, delirium, nausea and sometimes convulsions. Withdrawal from coffee or colas that contain caffeine (a stimulant) can produce depression, fatigue or headaches and may impair concentration. Withdrawal symptoms may last from two days to months, depending on the drug and the extent of addiction.
6. **Intoxication.** This term refers to the state of being under the influence of a drug with the effects ranging from stimulation to loss of consciousness. The intensity of this experience varies according to the drug, a person's physical reaction to the drug and other factors.
7. **Blackout.** This is the state of intoxication someone can reach using large quantities of alcohol.
   Similar to passing out, the intoxicated person remembers nothing that happened during the blackout. Unlike passing out, the intoxicated person in a blackout walks, talks and appears to know what he or she is doing.
8. **Trip.** This term describes an experience on a psychoactive drug, especially a hallucinogen such as LSD.
9. **Overdose.** An overdose is taking more than a safe amount of any drug.
   Reactions to an overdose range from nausea and vomiting to a loss of consciousness or death.
10. **Abstinence.** This term means choosing not to use drugs.
11. **Controlled substances.** Use of these drugs is regulated by law. It's either

against the law for people to use them (for example, LSD), or they can be purchased only with a doctor's prescription.

12. **Over-the-counter drugs.** People can buy medicine such as aspirin, diet pills and and allergy medications without a prescription.

    Use of these drugs isn't always harmless. People need to read labels carefully. They should also check with their doctor or druggist if they use a medication over a long period of time.

Psychoactive drugs. The following descriptions and definitions are grouped according to the effects psychoactive drugs have on the mind and central nervous system. These descriptions and definitions can help parents and kids understand the effects of these powerful drugs that produce changes in feelings, thoughts, perceptions and behavior.

1. **Narcotics.** "Narcotic" comes from the Greek word meaning stupor. Narcotics derived from the opium poppy include heroin, a highly addictive powder that's injected, smoked or snorted; morphine, a white powder usually injected for pain; and codeine, a less powerful form used in cough medications. There are also non-opiate, synthetic narcotics such as Methadone and Demerol.

   Narcotics are controlled substances. People use these drugs for pain relief, tranquilization, sedation and to induce sleep. Narcotics affect the central nervous system, but through it affect many other organs and systems. Using narcotics to relieve anxiety is not only dangerous but can lead to drug addiction.

2. **Depressants.** Called "downers," depressants affect the nervous system, producing relaxation, sleep and pain relief. Barbiturates, the largest class of depressants, are usually available in capsules or tablets. Even though barbiturates are controlled substances, they're sold on the street as Amytal, Seconal and Nembutal.

   Other downers that aren't barbiturates include forms of methaqualone called Quaaludes or "Ludes" and chloral hydrate, used as a "Mickey Finn," or knockout drops. These depressants are also controlled substances.

   The most widely used depressant is alcohol, which isn't a controlled substance. It's the #1 drug choice among young people and adults. In small doses alcohol relaxes the body. In larger doses, it impairs judgment and motor coordination. Consuming excess amounts of alcohol can cause death.

   Doctors prescribe some depressants (such as Valium and Librium) in small doses to relieve anxiety and muscle tension. Larger doses can produce effects similar to large doses of alcohol such as slurred speech, loss of motor coordination and impaired judgment. Combining a depressant with alcohol is extremely dangerous because the combined effects are unpredictable and vary from person to person and time to time.

3. **Stimulants.** These drugs excite the central nervous system, resulting in elevated blood pressure, increased alertness, increased muscle performance and euphoria.

   Cocaine is a highly addictive, illegal white powder extracted from the coca plant. This powder can be snorted, smoked or injected. Its stimulating effects produce euphoria and overconfidence. Physicians believe cocaine is the most addictive drug.

   Suppliers have developed another form of cocaine called "crack." By processing the cocaine powder into pieces resembling white gravel or soap chips to be smoked, they've created an even more addictive product that's affordable for people of all ages and backgrounds. For example, crack rocks cost about one-tenth as much as a gram of cocaine.

   Amphetamines ("speed") are man-made stimulants that may have longer-lasting effects than cocaine. Commonly used amphetamines are Benzedrine, Dexedrine and Methedrine.

   Amphetamine abusers are usually seeking a euphoric feeling. Amphetamines are widely used to stave sleepiness and to suppress the appetite. Long-term abusers often suffer from malnutrition because they don't eat properly.

Continued or unsupervised use of amphetamines is dangerous because these drugs elevate blood pressure and use the body's natural energy reserves.

Nicotine is an active stimulant present in all forms of tobacco. Smoking this highly addictive drug not only increases the heart rate but can also predispose the body to serious diseases of the lungs, heart and blood vessels.

The most commonly used stimulant is caffeine, found in coffee, cola and chocolate. Even though it's used in small doses, caffeine can be addicting in these products.

4. **Hallucinogens.** Most of these mind-altering drugs cause hallucinations—experiences in which individuals hear voices or see visions that aren't real. Hallucinogens also stimulate the central nervous system, increase brain activity and cross the senses (for example, a sound may be seen).

   The most potent hallucinogen is LSD (lysergic acid diethylamide), taken orally in liquid drops or tablets. In the '60s and early '70s, people experimented with LSD because they thought it opened their minds to creativity or aided spiritual searching. Some people had unpleasant or frightening experiences with this drug, and its popularity faded.

   "Magic mushrooms," another group of hallucinogens, contain the psilocybin fungus. Taken orally, the drug in these mushrooms react as a less potent form of LSD. Some Native Americans use this drug in their religious ceremonies.

   PCP, called "angel dust" or the "peace pill," is used as a veterinary anesthetic. This powerful drug is snorted or mixed with marijuana and smoked, but is also sold in tablet or powder form. PCP causes decreased sensitivity to pain and a rubbery feeling in the legs with impaired coordination. Mood disorders, anxiety and unusual behavior are other effects. Many people injure themselves on this drug.

5. **Cannabis.** Marijuana is the most popular form of this illegal drug within the United States. Marijuana cigarettes are made with the crushed leaves of the hemp plant and are referred to as "grass," "pot" or a "reefer." Marijuana is usually smoked and can be eaten. Scientists have identified 450 known chemicals in marijuana. The effects of using this drug include euphoria, relaxation, perceptual distortion, decreased ability to concentrate and impaired memory.

   The active ingredient in marijuana is THC (tetrahydrocannabinol). Marijuana growers have found ways to increase the amount of this ingredient, and today marijuana is up to 20 times stronger than it was 10 years ago. The chemicals in marijuana stay in the body for a month or more.

   One of parents' and teachers' main concerns about young people's marijuana use is its impact on motivation and cognition. Marijuana can also produce paranoia and psychosis. Although not physically addictive, marijuana is a mind-altering drug. Long-term use can damage the lungs and alter the reproductive functions. Once thought to be harmless, marijuana is now recognized as harmful in its short- and long-term effects.

6. **Inhalants.** These chemicals give off vapors and produce intoxication when inhaled. Inhalants may cause confusion, excitement and sometimes hallucinations. These toxic vapors can cause physical problems such as bone marrow, heart, brain and liver damage.

   To get high, individuals may place products like solvents, cleaning fluids, paint, glue or aerosols inside a bag or on a cloth and inhale them. Manufacturers know there's no safe way to inhale these vapors and label products with strong warnings not to inhale them.

7. **Deliriants.** These drugs are derived from a group of plants with strange smells and peculiar flowers. They're used to induce an altered state of consciousness. Physical side effects may include nausea, dizziness, headaches and prostration. Mental side effects may vary from confusion and disorientation to a vivid hallucination.

Youth Track—Activity 2 Handout
Parent Track—Activity 3 Handout

"What Do You Know About Drugs?" Crossword Puzzle

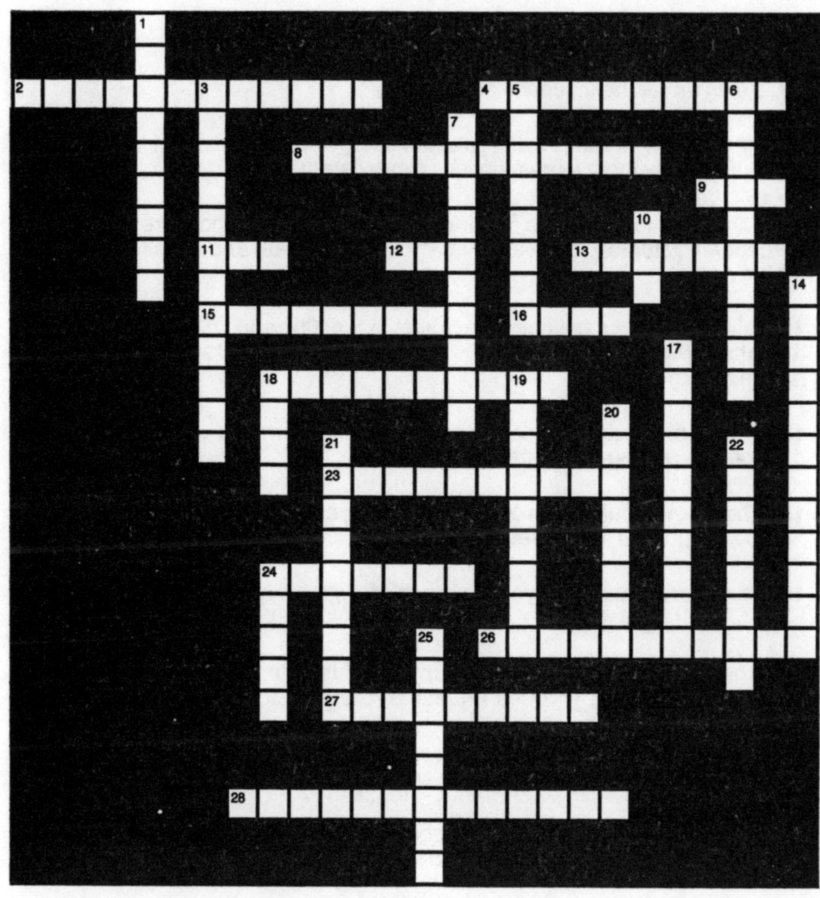

(Clues for Crossword Puzzle on next two pages)

continued

"What Do You Know About Drugs?"

(Clues for Crossword Puzzle)

Across

2. Drugs grouped according to the effects they have on the mind and central nervous system

4. Choosing not to use drugs

8. Being under the influence of a drug

9. Drugs such as aspirin, diet pills and allergy medications that individuals can purchase without a prescription (abbreviated)

11. The active ingredient in marijuana that produces euphoria, relaxation, perceptual distortion, decreased ability to concentrate and impaired memory (abbreviated)

12. The most potent hallucinogen; used in the '60s and '70s because people thought the drug opened their minds to creativity or aided spiritual searching (abbreviated)

13. The most widely used depressant; it isn't a controlled substance; the #1 drug choice among young people and adults

15. The most popular form of the illegal drug cannabis; referred to as "grass," "pot" or a "reefer"

16. An experience on a psychoactive drug, especially a hallucinogen such as LSD

18. Chemicals derived from a group of plants with strange smells and peculiar flowers that produce an altered state of consciousness

23. Means an individual regularly uses a drug and relies on it for performing normal activities

24. A highly addictive, illegal white powder extracted from the coca plant; its stimulating effects produce euphoria and overconfidence

26. Called downers; in small doses these drugs relieve anxiety and muscle tension; larger doses can produce effects similar to those of excessive alcohol consumption (slurred speech, loss of motor coordination and impaired judgment)

27. Controlled substances used to relieve pain, tranquilize, sedate and induce sleep; the derivatives from the opium poppy include heroin, morphine, and codeine; non-opiate forms include Methadone and Demerol

28. Mind-altering drugs that stimulate the central nervous system, increase brain activity and cause the user to hear voices or see visions that aren't real

continued

Down

1. Chemicals that give off vapors and produce intoxication when inhaled; may cause confusion, excitement and sometimes hallucinations

3. Man-made stimulants called "speed" sometimes prescribed for weight control; may have longer-lasting effects than cocaine; common examples include Benzedrine, Dexedrine and Methedrine

5. When individuals use large quantities of alcohol, they can reach a state of intoxication in which they walk, talk and appear to know what they're doing, but later remember nothing

6. Drugs regulated by law; these substances are either against the law for anyone to use or they can be purchased only with a doctor's prescription

7. The physical symptoms a person experiences when trying to readjust to living without a drug

10. A veterinary anesthetic; produces decreased sensitivity to pain, impaired coordination, mood disorders, anxiety and unusual behavior; called "angel dust" or the "peace pill" (abbreviated)

14. Used to relieve anxiety and induce sleep; common examples of these depressants include Amytal, Seconal and Nembutal; rarely addictive

17. Drugs that excite the central nervous system, resulting in elevated blood pressure, increased alertness, increased muscle performance and euphoria

18. A chemical that, even in small doses, can produce significant changes in the body and mind

19. When the body learns to adjust to the presence of a drug, the body has reached a level of ____________________

20. To take more than a safe amount of any drug

21. Physical dependence on a drug

22. The most commonly used stimulant, found in coffee, cola and chocolate; it can be addictive

24. A new, highly addictive, affordable form of cocaine made by processing the powder into pieces resembling white gravel or soap chips to be smoked

25. The active ingredient in all forms of tobacco; a highly addictive stimulant

Youth Track—Activity 3 Handout

Why Drugs?

Instructions: Fill in the blanks with the information assigned to your pair. Then brainstorm alternative ideas on how people can meet their needs without using drugs.

Reason people use drugs:

Needs reflected by this reason:

Alternatives to drug use:

Youth Track—Activity 4 Handout

How Does Drug Use Affect Me?

Instructions: Answer the following questions about yourself.

1. What are your needs?

2. What's one reason you might consider using a drug?

3. Without your parent's permission, would you use over-the-counter drugs? prescription drugs? illegal drugs? Explain.

4. In what ways have you been affected by another person's drug use?

5. What alternatives to drug use work for you?

6. What questions do you still have about drugs?

Instructions: The "At-Home Track 3" offers junior highers and parents an opportunity to discuss the issue studied in this session. Set aside 30 minutes for this meeting.

Before you begin, remember to listen as well as talk. Arguments or put-downs don't encourage conversation. Defensiveness or shouting doesn't encourage growth or change.

Now go ahead with this meeting. Follow directions and make new discoveries about yourself and other family members.

Self-esteem booster: I'm a caretaker of God's creations. I must use his creations wisely.

Sharing time: To begin this time together,

Parent: Talk with your young person about how you want to work with him or her to meet his or her needs.

Junior higher: Ask your parent any questions you have about drugs.

Bible study: Read Romans 12:1-2 together. "Therefore, I urge you, brothers, in view of God's mercy, to offer your bodies as living sacrifices, holy and pleasing to God—this is your spiritual act of worship. Do not conform any longer to the pattern of this world, but be transformed by the renewing of your mind. Then you will be able to test and approve what God's will is—his good, pleasing and perfect will." Answer the following questions:

1. What does this passage say to you?
2. How can you apply this passage to your life or your family?

Activity: Spend an evening together watching a favorite television program. Then discuss the following questions:

1. What messages about drugs does this program or its commercials convey?
2. What's your favorite movie? What messages about drugs does it convey?
3. What media person do you admire (a sports hero, actor, actress, musician or political leader)? What messages about drugs does this person model?
4. How do the media messages about drugs affect your life? What messages about drugs do you model for others?

A plan of action: Set aside some time to look at the TV schedule and the movie listings. Check your favorites, then talk about what messages they convey about drug use. If you aren't sure, watch the programs together.

Close this time together by talking about one thing you learned from one another during this meeting.

SESSION 4

My Body Belongs to God

Young people are becoming increasingly conscious of what they're doing to their bodies. When they also realize that their bodies are gifts from God, they're even more concerned about how they treat this special possession. But differing values and misunderstandings about certain chemicals' effects on the body contribute to confusion about what to do about drugs. Young people must learn to make educated decisions about how to glorify God with their bodies.

Objectives

In this session junior highers and parents will:

- find out ways individuals glorify God with their bodies.
- read Bible passages that offer drug-use guidelines.
- discuss six factors that influence a person's relationship to a drug.
- evaluate drug relationships experienced in various scenarios.
- complete a chemical health assessment.

Supplies

- ☐ newsprint
- ☐ masking tape
- ☐ pencils
- ☐ photocopies of "Drug Information" handout from Session 3
- ☐ Bibles

"Youth Track" only

- ☐ water-based markers

"Parent Track" only

- ☐ 3×5 cards

PREPARATION

Read the session and photocopy the handouts.

Before the meeting, write the following "Self-esteem booster" on newsprint and tape it onto the wall: "I can glorify God with the body God gave me."

Know what your church teaches about drug use before you begin this session. If you aren't sure, check with your minister rather than give false information.

Tape a sheet of newsprint onto the wall. Label it "Ways I Glorify God With My Body" (Activity #2).

Copy the "Six Factors That Influence a Person's Relationship to a Drug" diagram on newsprint. Tape this diagram onto the wall when indicated in Activity #5.

Six Factors That Influence a Person's Relationship to a Drug

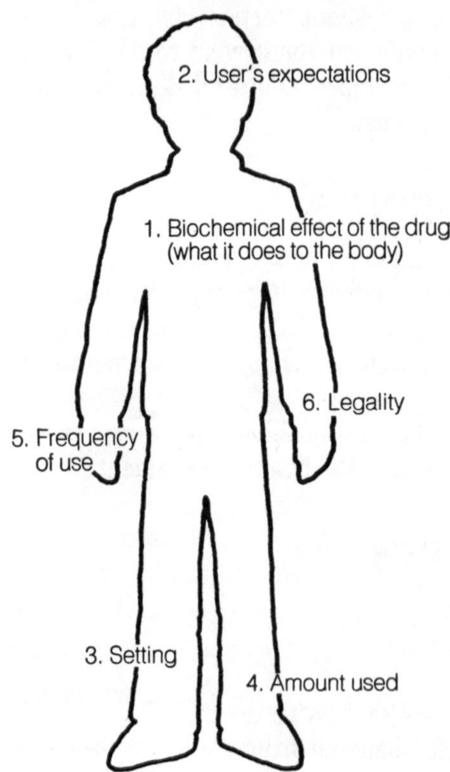

Have copies of the Session 3 "Drug Information" handout available for participants' reference (Activity #5).

Youth Track only: Tape a sheet of newsprint onto the wall. Label it "The Harmful Consequences of Drug Use" (Activity #5).

Parent Track only: Tape a blank sheet of newsprint onto the wall (Activity #3).

SESSION ACTIVITIES

1. Opening—Respond to participants' questions or comments about the last session or the "At-Home Track 3" handout.

Answer questions about drugs from the last session. Ask if participants have any other questions about drugs. Answer those or agree to look for answers before the next session.

2. Pantomime—Ask participants to form a circle. Have them each take turns pantomiming something they do that glorifies God with their body. One person may pantomime swimming, while another may pretend to sing. Other individuals might pantomime guitar playing, exercising, reading or praying.

Have everybody guess what each person is doing. List these talents or abilities on the newsprint labeled "Ways I Glorify God With My Body."

Youth Track

3. Biblical guidelines—Say: "We've talked about ways we glorify God with our bodies. Now it's important to learn what the Bible says about our bodies and how we should relate to drugs.

"Remember, the Bible doesn't mention specific drugs except wine or strong drink. Therefore, we need to apply the directions to other drugs."

Parent Track

3. What does the Bible say?—Say: "All of us have different ways we glorify God with our bodies. Our kids are the same. Since no two people are alike, people may choose to glorify God in a way that's totally their own.

"It's important to examine what the Bible says about our bodies and how we should glorify God. It's also important to

Youth Track

Parent Track

find out how we should relate to drugs. Since the Bible doesn't mention specific drugs except wine or strong drink, we need to apply the Bible's directions to other drugs."

Ask participants to form groups of four. Give each group a Bible and assign each group one of the following scripture passages: Deuteronomy 29:2-6; Luke 1:11-17; John 2:1-11; 1 Corinthians 10:31-33; and Ephesians 5:15-20.

Youth Track

Give each group newsprint and markers. Ask each group to design a poster illustrating its biblical passage. For example, if a group were assigned Romans 14:21, group members might create a poster saying, "If it would cause your brother or sister to fall . . ." Then they could draw examples or write words that might influence another person's behavior (such as a person taking a drink). Have kids think of other actions that might influence another person's behavior such as cursing, fighting or sniffing an inhalant.

After groups complete their posters, have a volunteer from each group read aloud the group's scripture passage and explain its poster to the total group. Ask small group members to tape their posters onto the wall.

Parent Track

Give each small group a photocopy of the "What Does the Bible Say?" handout. Ask group members to be prepared to talk about their responses to the discussion questions with the total group.

Have volunteers read their scripture passages to the whole group and discuss their responses to the first five questions. Instruct groups to answer questions or respond to disagreements others might have.

On the blank sheet of newsprint, list parents' ideas about what your church teaches about drug use. Clarify any misunderstandings.

4. Appropriate drug use—Talk about the diversity among cultures and Christian groups regarding appropriate drug use.

Say: "Making decisions about appropriate drug use varies widely among cultures. Different cultures make different value judgments about drugs. Generally among Caucasian Americans, social use of alcohol is approved and use of psychoactive drugs meets with strong disapproval. Some American Indians, however, use peyote (a natural hallucinogen) in religious rituals but consider alcohol a curse.

"Christian groups also disagree about appropriate drug use. For example, most Catholics sanction alcohol for socializing, while Seventh-Day Adventists believe it's wrong to have even one drink. Some denominations serve wine for communion, while others substitute grape juice or another non-alcoholic drink. Most Protestant groups use drugs for physical healing, yet some Christians refuse drugs and rely solely on prayer for healing. All Christians must choose how to use drugs appropriately within their particular set of values.

"There are many references to wine and strong drink in the Bible. Although other drugs aren't mentioned, the Old and New Testament references to wine and the body can help individuals decide about drug use. First, the New Testament tells Christians their bodies are 'temples of the Holy Spirit' (1 Corinthians 3:16-17; 6:19-20). Their bodies belong to God and they are to glorify God with their bodies. God's presence in people's bodies should influence people's decisions about drug use. Christians should treat their bodies, God's temples, with respect and loving care.

"Second, the Old and New Testaments portray wine as part of God's creation and acceptable for God's people (Exodus 29:40; Deuteronomy 32:14; Psalm 104:15; Isaiah 25:6). The Israelites used wine as an offering and as part of their celebrations. Jesus turned water into wine at a wedding feast (John 2:1-11) and used wine to symbolize the new covenant (Matthew 26:28-29).

"Third, the Bible speaks strongly against overindulgence of wine (Proverbs 20:1; Romans 13:13; Ephesians 5:18) and refers to abstinence as a viable choice in certain situations. God instructed certain people such as John the Baptist (Luke 1:15) not to use wine. Priests were forbidden to use wine in the Tent of Meeting (Leviticus 10:8-9). And pregnant women were forbidden to use wine (Judges 13:4).

"Because of differing value judgments about drugs, understanding drug use is a complicated challenge. Individuals must decide what constitutes chemical health, abuse and addiction. As caretakers of the chemicals and bodies God has created, people must act wisely to make sure use of chemicals, or drugs, doesn't adversely affect their minds, bodies, emotions, spirituality or relationships."

5. Six factors—Tape the "Six Factors That Influence a Person's Relationship to a Drug" diagram onto the wall.

Say: "One helpful way to differentiate between chemical health and abuse is to look at the relationship to a drug individuals develop. Each drug has a specific biochemical effect that's roughly the same with most people. Because individuals' body chemistries differ, however, identical amounts of the same drug can affect people differently. For example, a large person may not be affected by the same amount of alcohol as a smaller person.

"Drug users' expectations, or 'set,' may also affect how drugs alter people's moods and minds. For example, if an individual expects to get drunk on two beers, he or she is more likely to have that experience than the friend who expects to maintain control after two beers. A young person learns what to expect by listening to friends and from personal experience.

"Another factor that influences a person's relationship to a drug is the setting or environment in which the drug is used. This includes the immediate environment and the larger culture. For example, an American Indian whose culture chooses to use peyote in a religious ritual with his or her family will probably experience the effects of the drug differently than a young person who uses the drug to get high at a party with friends. The amount and number of times the drug is used are other important factors.

"Another obvious but important part of maintaining a healthy relationship to a drug is to obey society's laws. Breaking the law produces guilt and social alienation. It forces individuals to lie about their behavior, and lying creates tension. Social well-being isn't possible when individuals break society's laws. Therefore, maintaining a healthy relationship to a drug involves wise use within the limits of the law. For young people, then, abstinence from alcohol and controlled substances is a healthy choice advocated by laws governing minors."

Read aloud the "Six Factors That Influence a Person's Relationship to a Drug'' and explain each one. For example, you could explain in the following way the effects of caffeine since it's present in colas and chocolate most junior highers enjoy.

1. Caffeine is a stimulant to the body.

2. The person who uses caffeine expects a high, at least in mental alertness or extra energy.

3. If moderate amounts of caffeine are used in a social setting, nervousness or jittery feelings may not be noticeable. Eating or drinking the same amount of caffeine alone may produce the same physical reaction, but it may be more obvious when no one else is around.

4. Too much caffeine depends upon an individual's tolerance level; however, two 12-ounce colas definitely stimulate the senses.

5. If cola or chocolate is used indiscriminately, sleeplessness or nervousness may occur.

6. Caffeine is legal, readily available and is sometimes a hidden ingredient in foods or beverages.

Youth Track

Have kids choose another drug and discuss the six factors in relation to that drug. Use the information in Session 3 to help them find information they don't know. Encourage group members to discuss how drug use influences family, friends, school, legal responsibilities, finances, work, personal lives and spiritual experiences. Write group members' ideas on the newsprint labeled ''The Harmful Consequences of Drug Use.''

Parent Track

Have parents meet again in their groups of four. Ask each group to choose a drug besides caffeine and discuss the six factors in relation to that drug. (To make sure each group selects a different drug, ask someone from each small group to let you know what drug the group selected.) Have copies of the drug information from the last session available if parents need it. Encourage parents to discuss how drug use influences family, friends, school, legal responsibilities, finances, work, personal lives and spiritual experiences.

Give each group a sheet of newsprint and markers. Have

Youth Track

Parent Track

parents work together to create a poster about the drug they selected. Ask group members to tape their posters onto the wall and explain them to the total group.

6. Responsible drug use—Read aloud the following definitions of chemical health, chemical abuse and chemical addiction.

Chemical health is a state of well-being that exists in which responsible decisions are made about chemical use.

Chemical abuse is the continued use of a chemical despite adverse, destructive effects on health, behavior or relationships.

Chemical addiction is physical and psychological dependence on a chemical characterized by loss of control, tolerance, withdrawal and interference in social or school relationships. Addiction means enslavement to a chemical.

Give each participant a pencil and photocopy of the "Guidelines for Using Drugs Responsibly" handout.

Read aloud the "Guidelines for Using Drugs Responsibly." Ask kids to talk about how junior highers could use each guideline. Have kids list other practical suggestions.

7. Scenarios—Have participants meet again in their small groups. Ask each group to choose a discussion leader and a recorder. Give each group recorder a marker and newsprint. Say: "The task for each of your groups is to decide what kind of relationship the person in the scenario has to the drug that's mentioned. Use the 'Six Factors That Influence a Person's Relationship to a

Have parents read the guidelines individually and ask themselves how their junior highers could use each guideline. Have parents list other practical suggestions for their kids.

7. Scenarios—Give each group a photocopy of the "Scenarios" handout. Ask parent volunteers to read each of the scenarios. After each reading, have parents discuss the scenario to determine what kind of relationship the person has with the drug that's mentioned. Remind parents to use the "Six Factors That Influence a Person's Relationship to a Drug" and the "Guidelines for

Youth Track

Drug' and the 'Guidelines for Using Drugs Responsibly' to evaluate the person's relationship with the drug."

Give discussion leaders each a photocopy of the "Scenarios" handout and ask them to read aloud the scenarios one at a time to their group. While group members discuss the scenarios, have group recorders list the discussion's main points. When groups finish, have recorders report to the total group the group's decision about the person's relationship to the drug.

Parent Track

Using Drugs Responsibly" as a basis for their discussions.

8. Chemical health assessment—Give each participant a photocopy of the "Chemical Health Assessment" handout. Ask individuals to list drugs they know junior highers use and answer the questions about each drug.

Have individuals talk about their list with the rest of the group and encourage them to answer one another's questions.

Youth Track

9. Closing—Ask participants to form a circle. Give each person a water-based marker. Say: "Each of you has ways you glorify God with your body. On the inside of your palm, write 'I'll glorify God by . . .' and complete the sentence. Share your idea with the people on both sides of you."

Ask participants to join hands and pray silently for the individuals on both sides and their efforts to glorify God with their bodies. Close the meeting with

Parent Track

9. Closing—Give each parent a 3×5 card. Say: "Each of you is aware of ways your junior highers glorify God with their bodies. On this card, write a note to your young person telling how proud you are of the way your son or daughter uses his or her body to glorify God. Take this card home to show your junior higher during the 'At-Home Track.' "

Ask parents to form a circle and close with the following prayer: "God, we realize you

Youth Track

the following prayer: "God, we realize you created our bodies. We know you care about us and how we take care of ourselves. Help us realize how valuable we are in your eyes, and give us the strength to glorify you with everything we do. In Jesus' name, amen."

Parent Track

created us and our children. We know you care about all of us and how we take care of our bodies. Help us acknowledge one another's value and give us the strength to glorify you in everything we do. In Jesus' name, amen."

Distribute photocopies of the "At-Home Track 4" handout. Explain that this handout should be completed by each junior higher and his or her parent before the next session. Encourage kids or parents to schedule a time for this at-home meeting as soon as possible.

Parent Track—Activity 3 Handout

What Does the Bible Say?

Instructions: Read your assigned scripture passage and answer the following questions. Be prepared to tell your answers to the total group.

1. What does the Bible say about a person's body in this verse?

2. What does the Bible say about wine or strong drink in this verse?

3. What guideline for using wine or strong drink does the Bible offer in this situation?

4. How can you use this guideline in your decision-making regarding drug use?

5. How can you use this guideline to help your junior higher make good decisions about drug use?

6. What does your church teach regarding drug use?

Youth and Parent Tracks
Activity 6 Handout

◆ Guidelines for Using Drugs Responsibly ◆

Instructions: Read and discuss the following guidelines. In the space provided, write specific suggestions for using these guidelines.

To use drugs responsibly, a person should:

1. recognize the substance used as a drug and know what it does to the body. For example, a person who drinks cola should know that it contains caffeine that stimulates the senses.

2. continually experience the drug as useful. For example, if a person enjoys cola and finds that this drink provides a positive accompaniment to social situations without adverse consequences, that person is using the drug responsibly.

3. control the use of the drug. When people have a good relationship to a drug, they can take it or leave it. There's no dependence on regular use of the drug. For example, the individual who can drink colas or do without them and still socialize or get work done controls using the drug.

4. maintain freedom from a drug's harmful consequences. If a drug interferes with physical health, personal relationships with friends or family, progress at school or work, legal concerns, financial responsibilities or spirituality, then individuals are adversely affected by chemical use. When people use a drug despite harm to themselves, this constitutes drug abuse. For example, when an individual drinks excessive amounts of cola or has a cola close to bedtime, the caffeine's stimulation can disrupt motor functions or hinder sleep.

When individuals use drugs responsibly, they have a healthy relationship to drugs.

Youth and Parent Tracks
Activity 7 Handout

Scenarios

Scenario 1:

Betty, an eighth-grader, walks to school every day with her friends. She began smoking marijuana when she was 12 years old. She and her friends smoke a marijuana joint twice a week before starting the school day.

Betty says marijuana is an herb and except for the smoke, it doesn't hurt your body. She says she likes using it because her morning classes are boring and smoking pot makes school more fun for her.

Betty doesn't smoke marijuana every week; sometimes she goes several weeks without it. Betty's mother disapproves of smoking and doesn't know her daughter is using marijuana. Betty's younger brother thinks the situation is funny. Betty's best friend ended the relationship when Betty told her she'd continue using pot once in a while. But Betty's new friends encourage her to smoke.

Scenario 2:

Sam is a ninth-grader who wants to go to college. Although he's smart, he finds studying difficult and time-consuming. Sam likes to study late at night because it's quiet in his house. Two or three times a week, he drinks a cup of coffee at night and studies several hours. He says the coffee helps him study longer because the caffeine keeps him alert.

After several hours, Sam stops studying and goes to sleep about 2 a.m. He says he has no problem falling asleep. Sam doesn't drink coffee any other time because he doesn't really like it.

Sam admits he can study without coffee, but feels he's more productive with it. His grades reflect his extra work. Sam's parents aren't worried because he drinks coffee, but they're concerned because he stays up late during the week.

Scenario 3:

Bob, a seventh-grader, began smoking cigarettes when he was 11 years old. Knowing his parents wouldn't approve, Bob has his older brother buy cigarettes for him. Bob now smokes a pack a week. Most of his friends tell him he should quit, but he's not worried. He knows he can quit smoking any time he wants.

Scenario 4:

Alice finally has been accepted by the "in" group in her junior high. She's attended several parties and has joined her new friends for most of their activities. At the last party some of the group asked if she wanted to "snort a line of coke." Unsure what they meant, she refused but said she'd like to watch. Her best friend and three other kids inhaled the white powder and seemed relaxed and happy the rest of the evening.

Alice is debating whether to say yes the next time someone asks. She'd like to relax around the boys so she could talk to them without being so nervous. But she also knows that using coke (cocaine) is against the law and she could get into trouble if anyone found out.

Youth and Parent Tracks
Activity 8 Handout

Chemical Health Assessment

Instructions: List the drugs junior highers use such as caffeine, nicotine or marijuana. Then answer the questions about each drug.

Drugs People Use	What does it do to their bodies?	How often do they use this drug?	How much do they use?	What are the harmful consequences?
Example: CAFFEINE	STIMULATES SENSES, HIGH BLOOD PRESSURE	FOUR TO SIX TIMES A DAY	ONE TO TWO CUPS OF COLA OR COFFEE AT A TIME	IT MAKES THEM JITTERY, IRRITABLE, NERVOUS

Instructions: The "At-Home Track 4" offers junior highers and parents an opportunity to discuss the issue studied in this session. Set aside 30 minutes for this meeting.

Before you begin, remember to listen as well as talk. Arguments or put-downs don't encourage conversation. Defensiveness or shouting doesn't encourage growth or change.

Now go ahead with this meeting. Follow directions and make new discoveries about yourself and other family members.

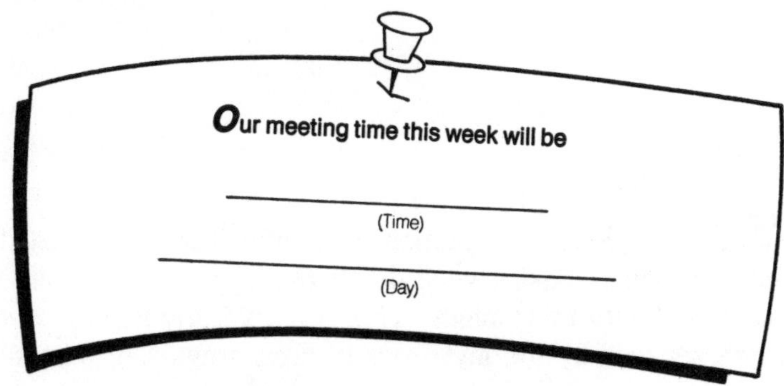

Self-esteem booster: I can glorify God with the body God gave me.

Sharing time: To begin this time together,

Parent: Give your junior higher the note you wrote about how proud you are of how your young person uses his or her body to glorify God.

Junior higher: Talk with your parent about one way you want to glorify God with your body.

Bible study: Read 1 Corinthians 6:19-20 together. "Do you not know that your body is a temple of the Holy Spirit, who is in you, whom you have received from God? You are not your own; you were bought at a price. Therefore honor God with your body." Answer the following questions:

1. What does this passage say to you?
2. How can you apply this passage to your life or your family?

Activity: Eat a healthy meal and then go for a walk together. When you come back discuss the following questions:

1. Think of a person whose Christian faith you admire. What do you admire about his or her faith? How does this person glorify God with his or her body?
2. Do you know any people who are using drugs in an unhealthy, abusive or addictive way? If so, what harmful consequences do you see from this drug use? What can you do about it?
3. What three things can you do to take better care of your body?

A plan of action: Each person should choose one thing to do to take better care of his or her body. Tell the rest of the family how you're going to do this. Spend at least 30 minutes each day improving this area of your life. Plan a family celebration for the end of the week to glorify God.

For example, if you decide to get more exercise so you have more stamina, walk briskly for 30 minutes each day. At the end of the week, take a leisurely walk together to see how the rest of creation glorifies God.

SESSION 5

Decision-Making: Beyond Just Saying No

Young people face temptation constantly. They're confused and need guidance in making good decisions. They need to learn how to love God with their minds. This is particularly important when they're seduced by the mysteries of illicit drugs and must decide whether to use or refuse drugs.

Rather than make absolute judgments and use scare tactics, parents can offer their young people a helpful approach for making decisions about using drugs. Parents can begin by loving and respecting their young people. They can present accurate information about drugs—what these chemicals do and what constitutes abuse. With this kind of support and information, young people can develop chemical health by exploring their own values, assessing the risks and consequences of using drugs and using their decision-making skills.

NOTES TO THE LEADER

All young people at some point in their lives must decide whether to use or refuse drugs. Most kids make their first decision about drug use when faced with peer pressure. Or curiosity about drugs might cause some young people to seek friends who already use drugs. Some young people use drugs because they can't cope with the stresses in their lives.

Many young people don't know they're taking risks with potentially dangerous drugs. They use drugs without full awareness of short- or long-term effects.

Telling young people that all drugs are bad will only heighten their interest in this "forbidden fruit." Even though abstinence is a positive, viable choice for young people, trying to scare kids away from using drugs ignores the problem's complexities.

In this imperfect world, striving to do what's right and seeking to understand God's will isn't easy. All individuals face daily temptations and confusion about making appropriate decisions.

OBJECTIVES

In this session junior highers and parents will:

- discuss how to make good decisions about drugs.
- talk about values concerning drugs.
- make badges to symbolize qualities kids can develop in decision-making about drugs.

SUPPLIES

- ☐ newsprint
- ☐ markers
- ☐ masking tape
- ☐ pencils
- ☐ construction paper
- ☐ scissors
- ☐ candle with a holder
- ☐ matches
- ☐ TV set
- ☐ videocassette recorder
- ☐ blank videotape
- ☐ Bible

"Youth Track" only

- ☐ paper

PREPARATION

Read the session and photocopy the handouts.

Before the meeting, write the following "Self-esteem booster" on newsprint and tape it onto the wall: "I'm responsible for making healthy decisions about drugs."

Record popular TV commercials on the blank videotape.

Write the "Steps for Making a Good Decision" on newsprint and tape it onto the wall during Activity #4.

Steps for Making a Good Decision

1. Identify the problem or choice to be made.
2. Identify different solutions.
3. List the consequences of each solution (physical, emotional, legal and impact on friends or family).
4. Consider your values.
5. Decide what to do.

Youth Track only: Make three large newsprint signs: "Agree," "Disagree" and "I Don't Know." Tape them along one wall in that order (Activity #3).

Set up a table (Activity #5).

SESSION ACTIVITIES

1. Opening—Respond to participants' questions or comments about the last session or the "At-Home Track 4" handout. Answer any unanswered questions participants had about drugs during the last session.

Play videotaped TV commercials as participants arrive.

Youth Track

2. Making commercials—Have kids form groups of four. Say: "All of us are fascinated by certain TV commercials. What are your favorites? What specific things do you like about them? What grabs your attention? Why are they effective?"

After a brief discussion, ask each small group to create a TV commercial promoting a healthy drug-related decision or demonstrating the consequences

Parent Track

2. Looking back—Have parents think back to when they were in junior high and discuss the following questions.

- What were your greatest struggles?
- In what situations did you find it easy to say no?
- In what situations did you find it difficult to say no?
- How did you feel when you said no?
- In what situations does

Youth Track

of drug use. For example, one group might create a commercial discouraging cigarette use by interviewing the Marlboro man as he lies in a hospital bed with lung cancer. Another group might create a humorous musical commercial: "Using crack can make you crack." Have each group act out its commercial for the total group.

Parent Track

your young person have the most difficulty saying no?

3. Deciding values—Say: "In order to make healthy decisions about drugs, it's important to know our values. Values are our beliefs about what's right and wrong. As Christians, our values need to be in harmony with the values Christ lived."

Say: "Think about the following statements and stand next to the sign on the wall that reflects your opinion. After everyone takes a position, I'll ask everyone to talk with people who made the same choice about why they made that decision. Then I'll ask volunteers from the 'Agree' and 'Disagree' positions to explain to people in the 'I Don't Know' position why they made the decision they did. After the explanations people can make another choice."

Read the following "Value Statements" one at a time. Allow time for position statements after each one. Then give individuals a chance to change their positions.

Give each parent a pencil and photocopy of the "Drugs and Me: What Do I Think?" handout. Read aloud the instructions and give parents a few minutes to complete the handout.

Next have parents mark any of their responses their junior highers might not agree with. Ask parents to form groups of four and discuss responses their young people might not agree with. Encourage parents to help one another find ways to talk about these responses. For example, if a parent thinks his or her junior higher would be upset if a friend reported his or her drug use, other parents might offer suggestions such as talking to the young person

Youth Track

Value Statements

1. Alcohol is a beverage, not a drug.

2. Most kids use drugs because their friends push them to do it.

3. The drugs doctors give are safe because they're prescribed.

4. God's will for me is never to use any chemicals in my body.

5. Using alcohol is less dangerous than using LSD, heroin or marijuana.

6. If I'm careful, chemical use won't interfere with my relationship to God.

7. Adults shouldn't drink alcohol or use drugs that aren't prescribed by a doctor.

8. Most parents know less about drug abuse than the kids at school who use drugs.

9. Some kids get addicted to a drug because they use the drug too much.

10. If my best friend wanted me to try marijuana, I would.

11. It's okay to question adults' opinions when they talk about drugs.

12. Drugs help people deal with their problems.

13. If my parent drinks alcohol every day, drinking must be okay.

Parent Track

about what to do about drug use before it happens or using the report as a signal to watch for signs of drug use. Because of different parenting styles and backgrounds, parents each have their own ideas about how to handle each situation. But all ideas offer options for the parent looking for growth opportunities.

Youth Track

14. Kids can use drugs for fun if they're careful.

15. Using any drug except a prescribed drug is wrong.

16. If I thought about using any drug, I'd talk to my parent about it.

17. My parent should listen to my thoughts about drugs and care about what I think.

18. Non-Christians are more likely to use drugs destructively than Christians.

19. A true friend wouldn't tell my parent if I were using drugs.

Give each young person paper and a pencil. Say: "After listening to these value statements, write three value statements of your own about drugs. What three things do you think are okay or not okay about drug use? Include all kinds of drugs such as aspirin, caffeine, alcohol, marijuana, cocaine and LSD. These statements should reflect *your* values—not what others tell you to think."

When kids have written their value statements, have them meet in their groups of four to read them aloud. Ask:

- Did anyone in your group write a value statement that you agree with? What is that statement?

Parent Track

Youth Track

• Did anyone in your group write a value statement that you disagree with? Why do you disagree? How would you change that statement so the two of you could agree?

• Is it necessary for you to agree with everyone in your group? Why or why not?

4. Decision-making—Say: "You've talked about your values and drugs. Now you're going to make decisions based on your values and what you know about the consequences of drug use. For example, if you believe alcohol use is okay only for adults, you might encourage your friends to avoid it. This decision is based on a personal value. Or if you know that coffee contains a mild stimulant and believe it's helpful when used in moderation, you might decide to drink coffee before studying for a test. This decision is based on knowledge of what the drug does."

Parent Track

4. Decision-making—After parents discuss these suggestions and how to talk about drug use with their young people, say: "We've talked about values and drugs. Now we're going to talk about how to help young people make decisions based on their values and what they know about the consequences of drug use."

Say: "Decision-making is the process of making choices or arriving at solutions to problems. It's the act of using our intelligence and will to determine what to do." Tape the "Steps for Making a Good Decision" onto the wall and read it aloud to the group.

Youth Track

Then say: "Let's use these steps to make a decision about

Parent Track

Then say: "Use these steps to help your young person

Youth Track

the following situation: Your friend has invited you to a party. When you arrive, you find that the friend's parents aren't home and some kids are drinking beer. One kid opens a beer and hands it to you. What would you do?"

Use the "Steps for Making a Good Decision" to work through this situation. Help young people identify different solutions and the consequences of each. Help kids explore their decisions. Remember to avoid being judgmental. If kids have trouble talking, ask them to discuss the steps in their small groups and report results to the large group.

After a brief discussion, have kids form four groups. Give each group one of the "Situations" handouts and assign one situation to each group. Instruct groups to go through the "Steps for Making a Good Decision." When groups have made a decision, have them prepare a role play to illustrate their decision to the total group.

Remind participants to make a decision that promotes chemical health and avoids chemical abuse. After groups have performed their role play ask them to explain why they made that decision.

Parent Track

make a decision about the following situation: Your son or daughter has been invited to a party by a friend. When he or she arrives, the friend's parents are gone and some kids are drinking beer. One kid opens a beer and hands it to your child. How would you expect your young person to handle this situation? Put yourself in his or her place and work through the 'Steps for Making a Good Decision.' "

Help parents identify different solutions and the consequences of each solution. Encourage parents to explore each decision and relate it to their values. After exploring different solutions and consequences, ask parents to talk about the decision they think their child would make. Remind parents to avoid being judgmental.

After a brief discussion, have parents form four groups. Give each group a copy of the "Situations" handout and assign one situation to each group. Ask parents to consider the different solutions and consequences and decide what they should do as parents in each situation.

Youth Track

5. Badge-making—After participants have experienced good decision-making, put markers, scissors, tape and construction paper on a table. Say: "Making healthy decisions about using drugs requires using your brain. You need to be informed about drugs and think about all situations carefully.

"Making healthy decisions about drugs requires following your heart. You must remain loyal to your Christian beliefs and values.

"Making healthy decisions about drugs also requires emotional strength. You may be required to act with courage, to say no in situations where you'd feel more comfortable saying yes.

"Think about your decision-making. Which decision-making quality do you need to work on most—your brain, heart or emotional strength? Decide on the quality you need and make a badge that symbolizes that quality. For example, if you decide you need to work on your emotional strength, you might create a shield listing different things you can do to make a good decision."

After individuals have created their badges, have them put tape on the back and

Parent Track

5. Badge-making—Ask parents to remain in their four groups. Have them discuss the following questions:

- How do you discuss your values with your children?
- How do you model your values?
- What opportunities do you use to help your children develop decision-making skills?
- What are the expectations for drug use in your family? Are there consequences for not meeting these expectations? Explain.

Put markers, scissors, tape and construction paper on a table. Have parents make badges symbolizing the decision-making qualities they want to help their young people develop. Have parents put tape on the back of their badges and wear them. Ask them to talk about the meanings of their badges. Remind parents to take their badges home to share with their kids.

Youth Track

wear their badges. Ask them to explain why they created what they did. Remind kids to take their badges home to share with their parents.

6. Closing—Ask kids to form a large circle. Say: "We talked about decision-making. We discussed the qualities we need to help us make good decisions, and we've acknowledged those qualities we need to improve. Since each of us is responsible for making healthy decisions about drug use, let's affirm the qualities we see in one another that help us make good decisions."

Read aloud 1 John 1:5-7a and light the candle. Say: "As you pass this candle to the person on your right, tell which decision-making quality you appreciate most about that person. You might say, 'I appreciate your ability to think independently even when others try to get you to do what they want you to do.' "

After the affirmations, have participants each talk about one thing in this session that was important to them. Close the session with the following prayer: "God, thank you for giving us brains, hearts and the emotional strength to help us

Parent Track

6. Closing—Have parents form a circle. Read aloud 1 John 1:5-7a and light the candle. Say: "As you pass this candle to the person on your right, tell that person what decision-making quality you admire in him or her. Affirm this parent's ability to transmit that quality to his or her young person."

When every parent has been affirmed, close with the following prayer: "God, we know we're responsible for helping our kids make healthy decisions about drug use. Assure us of your presence as we strive to support and encourage our young people in their decision-making about drug use. Use us as instruments of your love and acceptance in their successes and failures. And give us the strength to remember our Christian values. In Jesus' name, amen."

Youth Track

make healthy decisions about drugs. Encourage us to support one another with our strengths and rely on you and one another in our weaknesses. Use us as instruments of your love and acceptance. In Jesus' name we pray, amen."

Parent Track

Distribute photocopies of the "At-Home Track 5" handout. Explain that this handout should be completed by each junior higher and his or her parent before the next session. Encourage kids or parents to schedule a time for this at-home meeting as soon as possible.

FOR SESSION 5

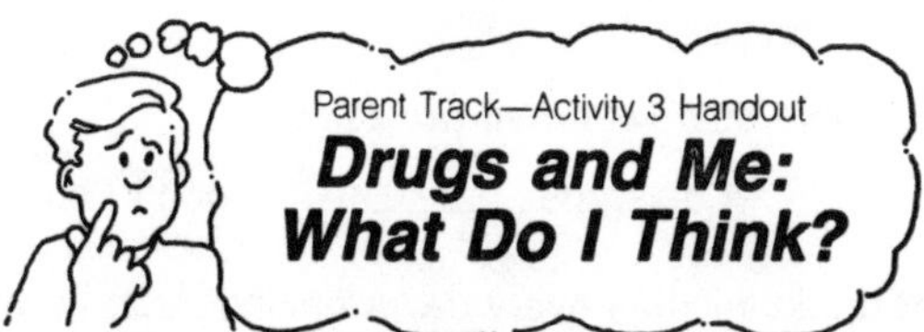

Parent Track—Activity 3 Handout

Drugs and Me: What Do I Think?

Instructions: Read each statement and write an "X" beside the response that reflects your values.

1. Alcohol is a beverage, not a drug.

I agree ________ I disagree ________ I don't know ________

2. Most kids use drugs because their friends push them to do it.

I agree ________ I disagree ________ I don't know ________

3. The drugs doctors give are safe because they're prescribed.

I agree ________ I disagree ________ I don't know ________

4. God's will for me is never to use any chemicals in my body.

I agree ________ I disagree ________ I don't know ________

5. Using alcohol is less dangerous than using LSD, heroin or marijuana.

I agree ________ I disagree ________ I don't know ________

6. If I'm careful, chemical use won't interfere with my relationship to God.

I agree ________ I disagree ________ I don't know ________

7. Adults shouldn't drink alcohol or use drugs that aren't prescribed by a doctor.

I agree ________ I disagree ________ I don't know ________

8. Most parents know less about drug abuse than the kids at school who use drugs.

I agree ________ I disagree ________ I don't know ________

9. Some kids get addicted to a drug because they use the drug too much.

I agree ________ I disagree ________ I don't know ________

10. If my best friend wanted me to try marijuana, I would.

I agree ________ I disagree ________ I don't know ________

11. It's okay to question adults' opinions when they talk about drugs.

I agree ________ I disagree ________ I don't know ________

continued

12. Drugs help people deal with their problems.

I agree ________ I disagree ________ I don't know ________

13. If my parent drinks alcohol every day, drinking must be okay.

I agree ________ I disagree ________ I don't know ________

14. Kids can use drugs for fun if they're careful.

I agree ________ I disagree ________ I don't know ________

15. Using any drug except a prescribed drug is wrong.

I agree ________ I disagree ________ I don't know ________

16. If I thought about using any drug, I'd talk to my parent about it.

I agree ________ I disagree ________ I don't know ________

17. My parent should listen to my thoughts about drugs and care about what I think.

I agree ________ I disagree ________ I don't know ________

18. Non-Christians are more likely to use drugs destructively than Christians.

I agree ________ I disagree ________ I don't know ________

19. A true friend wouldn't tell my parent if I were using drugs.

I agree ________ I disagree ________ I don't know ________

Youth Track—Activity 4 Handout

Situations

Instructions: Read the situation assigned to your group. Discuss how you would handle the situation, using the "Steps for Making a Good Decision."

#1 One of the brightest and most popular kids at school offers you a joint.

#2 Your best friend invites you to his birthday party. You find out his father is providing a keg of beer for the party.

#3 You've planned all week to go to a movie with your boyfriend. On the way to the movie the two of you decide to go to a party given by one of his friends. When you arrive, you find that people are using cocaine. When your boyfriend gets high, you try to decide whether to call home and ask your parents to pick you up at the boy's house or walk to the movie and pretend he left you there.

#4 The principal calls you into the office. When you arrive, you find your gym teacher, your parent and the principal waiting to talk with you about marijuana the gym teacher found in your locker. You realize the drug belongs to your best friend whose locker is next to yours.

Parent Track—Activity 4 Handout

Situations

Instructions: Read the situation assigned to your group. Discuss how you would handle the situation, using the "Steps for Making a Good Decision."

#1 Your 12-year-old son tells you he was offered a joint by one of the brightest and most popular kids at school.

#2 Your son asks if he can go to his best friend's birthday party. During your discussion you learn that the father of the best friend is providing a keg of beer for the party.

#3 Your daughter tells you she's going to a movie with her boyfriend. On the way to the movie the two of them decide to go to a party given by one of his friends. When they arrive, they learn that people are using cocaine. When her boyfriend gets high, your daughter calls and asks you to pick her up at the boy's house.

#4 The principal calls to ask you to come to the office. The gym teacher has found marijuana in your daughter's gym locker.

Instructions: The "At-Home Track 5" offers junior highers and parents an opportunity to discuss the issue studied in this session. Set aside 30 minutes for this meeting.

Before you begin, remember to listen as well as talk. Arguments or putdowns don't encourage conversation. Defensiveness or shouting doesn't encourage growth or change.

Now go ahead with this meeting. Follow directions and make new discoveries about yourself and other family members.

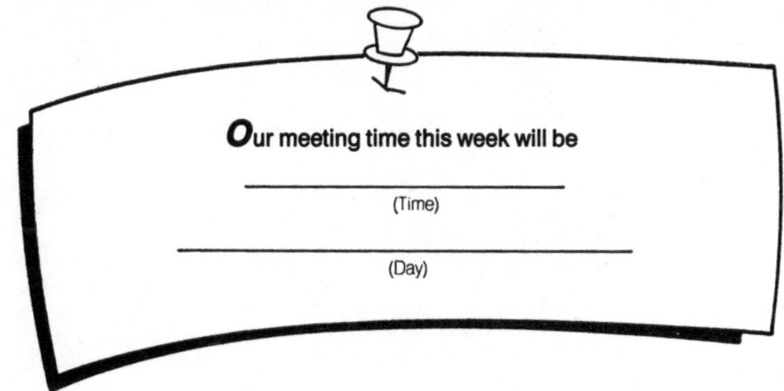

Self-esteem booster: I'm responsible for making healthy decisions about drugs.

Sharing time: To begin this time together,

Parent and junior higher: Talk about the badges you created. What decision-making skills do each of you need to develop? How can you help each other develop those skills?

Bible study: Read Philippians 3:13b-14 together. "But one thing I do: Forgetting what is behind and straining toward what is ahead, I press on toward the goal to win the prize for which God has called me heavenward in Christ Jesus." Answer the following questions:

1. What does this passage say to you?

2. How can you apply this passage to your life or your family?

Activity: As a family, discuss expectations and list rules about drug use. Situations you might include: attending a party where alcohol is served, riding in a car with an intoxicated driver, or smoking marijuana. Have everyone sign this list of rules to symbolize their support for one another as they struggle with decision-making.

continued

Rules

1.

2.

3.

4.

5.

We agree to follow these rules. We also agree to listen to one another when rules are broken. We also offer support for one another as we struggle with decision-making about drug use.

______________________ ______________________

______________________ ______________________

______________________ ______________________

______________________ ______________________

______________________ ______________________

______________________ ______________________

______________________ ______________________

A plan of action: Ask each family member to think about one problem he or she is struggling with. On separate nights during a week, have family members brainstorm solutions and consequences for each person's struggle. Encourage one another to think about values and offer support for one another as family members make decisions.

Close by saying the "Self-esteem booster" together. Then offer one another support in the areas each person wants to grow in. For example, if a young person needs to consider several solutions for a problem, the parent might respond, "I'll support you by helping you consider the different solutions without telling you what to do." Pray for each family member's ability to make good decisions.

SESSION 6

I Can Say No to Drugs and Still Have Friends

True friendship can be a wonderful gift and source of support in a changing world. When people are lonely, troubled, depressed or down on themselves, there's nothing as important as knowing there's a friend who genuinely cares.

Christians have that kind of friend in Jesus. Jesus offers people the greatest friendship in life. He cares for people so much that he gave his life for his friends. "Greater love has no one than this, that he lay down his life for his friends" (John 15:13). Young people and parents need to be reminded that Jesus is the friend they can always turn to in their changing lives. He serves as the perfect example of the genuine qualities of friendship.

OBJECTIVES

In this session junior highers and parents will:

- identify personal strengths or accomplishments.
- brainstorm a list of qualities participants value in friendship.
- participate in group exercises that demonstrate how peer pressure influences drug use.
- practice saying no in drug-related situations.
- discover alternatives to drug use.

SUPPLIES

- ☐ newsprint
- ☐ markers
- ☐ masking tape
- ☐ scissors
- ☐ pencils
- ☐ basket
- ☐ Bibles

"Youth Track" only

- ☐ different colors of construction paper
- ☐ cinnamon rolls

PREPARATION

Read the session and photocopy the handouts.

Before the meeting, write the following "Self-esteem booster" on newsprint and tape it onto the wall: "I can say no to drugs and still have friends."

Write the following friendship qualities from Barbara Varenhorst's book *Real Friends: Becoming the Friend You'd Like to Have* (Harper & Row) on newsprint and tape it onto the wall when indicated in Activity #2.

Real Friends Would . . .

1. Enjoy being around other people.
2. Respect, trust and value others for who they are, not for what they can offer.
3. Accept the faults of others, even if they dislike or disagree with their behavior.
4. Express and talk about their feelings openly.
5. Admit their own problems and faults.
6. Be aware of their own values.
7. Inconvenience themselves for another person.
8. Never take pleasure in making fun of someone or using put-downs that hurt.
9. Keep personal information private.
10. Speak up for what's best for themselves and the other person.
11. Know what their friend's values are.
12. Never pressure their friends to go against their values.

Make a photocopy of the "Scripture Cards" handout and cut the four cards apart (Activity #4).

Make a photocopy of the "Situations" handout and cut the six situations apart. Place a set of the six situations in the basket (Activity #6).

Youth Track only: Set up a table (Activity #7).

SESSION ACTIVITIES

1. Opening—Respond to participants' questions or comments about the last session or the "At-Home Track 5" handout.

Have participants form a circle and take turns sitting alone in the center. When a participant is in the center of the circle, others affirm him or her by noting strengths, physical attributes, a goal accomplished or a risk taken. After everyone has affirmed that person, have the group applaud. Ask another person to move to the center of the circle and continue until everyone has been affirmed. Ask:

- How did it feel to hear others acknowledge your strengths?
- How did you feel when everyone applauded?
- What was it like to clap for the other participants?
- What groups such as schoolmates, co-workers, family or friends give you positive feedback about your strengths or accomplishments?
- How can you encourage your friends or family members in their strengths?

2. What's in a friendship?—Give each person a pencil and photocopy of the "What's in a Friendship?" handout. Say: "Think about your best friend. What do you like about that person? What does that person do that makes him or her a good friend?" Read aloud the instructions and answer participants' questions.

Ask participants to form groups of four. Have them talk about the friendship qualities they identified. After a few minutes discuss qualities with the large group.

Tape the list of friendship qualities "Real Friends Would . . ." onto the wall. Tell the group this list includes qualities individuals might value in their friends or seek to develop in themselves.

After reading aloud and discussing these friendship qualities, say: "Developing these qualities in a friendship can be challenging but rewarding. Having friends who support your relationship eases life's stresses and helps you cope with troubles. Jesus is the kind of friend who never betrays his friendships."

Read aloud John 15:9-17. Then say: "On the back of your handout, draw a symbol of a friendship quality you appreciate about Jesus. Explain your symbol to the others in your small group."

After individuals draw and explain their symbols, ask, "Which of Jesus' friendship qualities would help people in a struggle against drug use?" As people name these qualities, have individuals who drew the symbols for these qualities tape their drawings onto the wall and label them.

Say: "We've talked about Jesus' friendship qualities that can help in a struggle against drug use. Think about the friendship qualities you and your friends possess that can help you face this same struggle.

"Listen as I read the following situations. Discuss the situation in your small groups and decide which friendship qualities would help in each situation." Read aloud each situation one at a time. Give groups two minutes to decide which friendship qualities would help in each situation.

- Your friend tells you that she's going to get drunk tonight.
- Your best friend is arrested for possessing marijuana.
- Some kids find a college student willing to help them purchase a keg of beer and they ask you to pitch in to help buy it.
- A friend shows you a large number of pills in a plastic bag and threatens to take them all because he's angry at what's happening in his life.

3. Pressure, pressure—After discussing the friendship qualities that would help in these situations, say: "Peer pressure operates as an invisible but powerful force, but not all peer pressure is destructive. In fact, many young people have friends who have a positive influence on others. These young people enjoy life and encourage those around them to enjoy it. These young people create a culture of their own without rejecting the culture of others. They choose unique hair styles, unusual clothes and strange music, but continue to appreciate others' choices, even their parents'. These kids encourage openness and like to talk with others about their ideas or opinions. When friends stray into negative experiences such as using drugs, these young people use their positive peer pressure to make friends take a look at their behavior. With positive peer pressure, they encourage these friends to make a positive choice—to be with friends who say no to drugs and reject a relationship with those who don't.

"Too often, however, we only hear about the peer pressure that encourages negative behavior. For example, many young people relate by putting each other down. This kind of negative peer pressure works on young people from the inside. In order to feel accepted by these peers, young people try to separate from their families and form their own identities. They try to adopt the attitudes and behaviors of the peer group that accepts them. And if this group introduces them to drugs, it's extremely difficult for kids to say no to these friends because they've identified with them."

Youth Track

Give each young person a photocopy of the "Shining Star" handout. Read aloud the instructions and ask kids to answer the questions by writing in the appropriate places on the star.

Answers might include: #1—went to church camp, helped in a youth group service project; #2—ditched school, smoked or drank, teased someone; #3—ignore it, explain why you won't do something, choose new friends, talk to parents; #4—didn't go to a party where there would be drinking, made friends with a new person at school, did homework when others were cheating; #5—

Parent Track

Give each parent a photocopy of the "Shining Star" handout. Ask parents to answer the questions for themselves by writing in the appropriate places on the star. Answers might include: #1—helped with a fund-raising drive, volunteered as a camp counselor; #2—bought new clothes that I didn't need, traded cars before I wanted to; #3—ignore it, explain why you won't do something, choose new friends; #4—didn't attend a party where I knew there'd be excessive drinking, refused to sign a neighborhood petition for something I didn't believe in; #5—often, sometimes, rare-

Youth Track

often, sometimes, rarely, never; center—to be accepted, to get invited to a big party, it's easier.

Parent Track

ly, never; center—to be accepted, to be recognized as successful, to fit into society.

Have group members each find a partner and talk about three answers from their stars. Ask individuals to tape their stars onto the wall.

Youth Track

Distribute photocopies of the "What's Your Pressure Rating?" handout. Read aloud the instructions and give everyone a few minutes to respond.

Parent Track

Distribute photocopies of the "What's Your Young Person's Pressure Rating?" handout. Read aloud the instructions and give everyone a few minutes to respond.

Discuss the results with the group by asking the following questions:

- What do young people do because of peer pressure?
- How is pressure from friends different from pressure from parents or God?
- What might happen if a person didn't give in to peer pressure in some of these areas? How could that affect the individual?

Have participants draw conclusions about whose pressures young people are most likely to respond to. Emphasize that most kids yield to peer pressure because they want to be accepted by others important to them.

4. Scripture cards—Ask participants to form four groups. Give each group a Bible and a photocopy of one of the "Scripture Cards." Assign each card to a different group. Say: "Follow the instructions on your card. Be prepared to have a volunteer tell the whole group what your small group discussed. Help the volunteer decide what to say."

Give groups time to read and discuss their scripture passages. After a few minutes have them read aloud their passages to the total group, and summarize their discussions and conclusions.

Youth Track

5. Ways to not give in— Say, "After listening to what God says about peer pressure, think about ways you can respond to this pressure without insulting or losing your friends." List participants' ideas on newsprint. Give each person a photocopy of the "Ways to Not Give In" handout. Read aloud the instructions and list of ideas. Discuss ideas participants don't understand or have questions about.

Parent Track

5. Ways to not give in— Say: "After listening to what God says about peer pressure, think about how you respond to this kind of pressure. Are you a good role model for your young person? How can people respond to peer pressure without insulting or losing friends?" List participants' ideas on newsprint.

Give each parent a photocopy of the "Ways to Not Give In" handout. Read aloud the instructions and list of ideas. Have parents discuss those ideas they don't understand or have questions about. Remind parents this list is written for young people, but parents may want to use the same ideas in their own lives. Encourage parents to take this handout home for the "At-Home Track 6."

6. Situations—Have participants meet in six groups. Ask each group to draw one of the "Situations" from the basket. Have each group read its situation and think of ways young people can respond to it without insulting or losing friends. Then have each group choose its favorite response and make up a short drama to perform for the total group. After each group performs its short drama, have the other groups applaud and suggest other responses that would work.

Encourage kids to be as honest as they can. Remind them it's okay to resist peer pressure, and it *is* possible to do so

Remind parents to encourage their kids to be as honest as they can. Parents should let kids know it's okay to resist

Youth Track

without losing friends. In fact, their resistance may help someone else do the same.

7. Closing—Place different colors of construction paper and markers on a table. Have kids make posters suggesting alternatives to drug use.

After a few minutes have kids bring their posters and make a circle. Read aloud Romans 12:2 to the group. Ask kids to explain their posters to the total group. Encourage them to take their posters home to show their parents.

Close the meeting with the following prayer: "God, thank you for friends. Thank you for these special relationships that mean so much to us. Give us the strength to resist peer pressure and the insight to find creative alternatives to drug use. Use us as positive influences within our peer groups. In the name of Jesus, the most positive influence we know, amen."

Have the kids lay their posters aside and join hands for a "cinnamon roll" hug. A young person at one end of the line is the "center" of the roll. The rest of the line wraps around

Parent Track

peer pressure, and it *is* possible to do so without losing friends. Parents should assure kids that their resistance may help someone else do the same.

7. Closing—Read Romans 12:2. Have parents think about specific ways they can be good role models for their young people. Ask them to talk about ways they say no to drug use such as avoiding caffeine or exercising instead of taking diet aids. List the alternatives they use on newsprint.

Close the meeting with the following prayer: "God, thank you for our young people and their friends. Thank you for these special relationships that mean so much to them. Give us the strength to help our young people resist peer pressure and the insight to help them find creative alternatives to drug use. Use us as positive influences with our children and within our peer groups. In the name of Jesus, the most positive influence we know, amen."

Youth Track	Parent Track
him or her, when everyone is wound up—squeeze! Serve cinnamon rolls for refreshments.	

Distribute photocopies of the "At-Home Track 6" handout. Explain that this handout should be completed by each junior higher and his or her parent before the next session. Encourage kids or parents to schedule a time for this at-home meeting as soon as possible.

FOR SESSION 6

Youth and Parent Tracks
Activity 2 Handout

What's in a Friendship?

Instructions: Inside the silhouette draw symbols that represent meaningful friendship qualities. Use symbols such as a ring (never-ending), pillow (supportive) or beach ball (fun to be around).

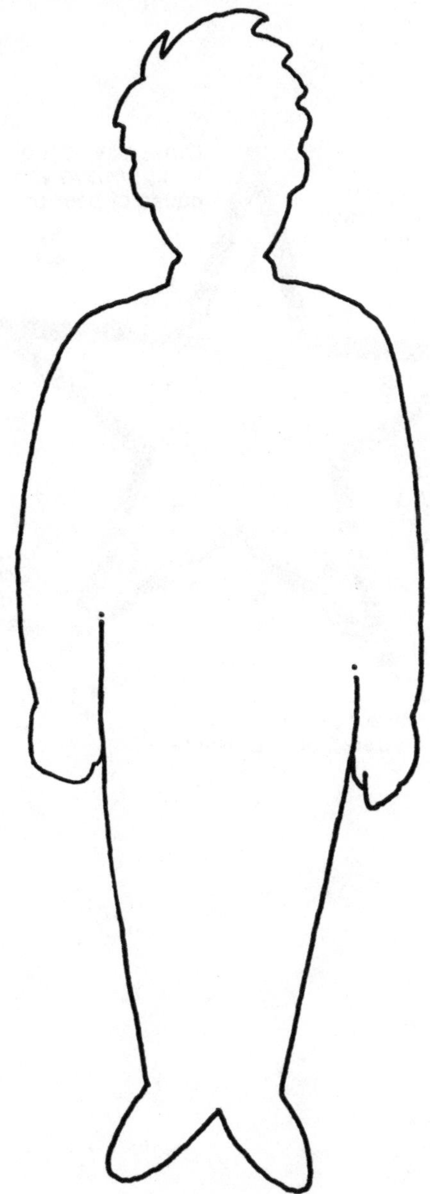

Youth and Parent Tracks
Activity 3 Handout

Shining Star

Instructions: Move in the direction of the arrows. Write your answers in the appropriate places on the star.

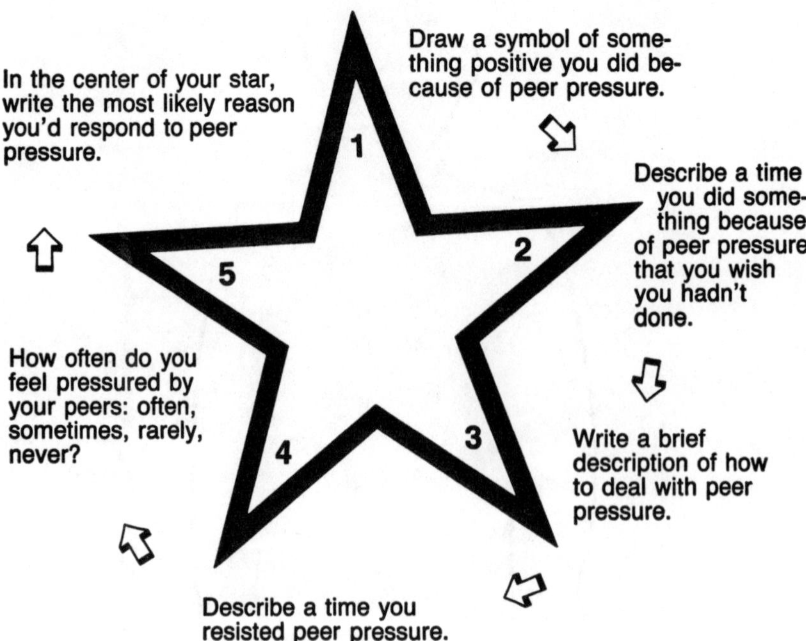

Youth Track—Activity 3 Handout

What's Your Pressure Rating?

Instructions: Below are situations in which people feel pressured to behave certain ways. Read each situation and think about what you'd do. Decide whose pressure you'd respond to and check the appropriate boxes. Not all responses fit all situations. You may have more than one checkmark for some situations and no checkmarks for other situations.

	I	my best friend	a group of friends	my parents	God	
1. I'd wear my hair a certain way because						expected me to.
2. I'd buy a certain brand of clothing because						expected me to.
3. I'd go to a party with someone I didn't really like because						expected me to.
4. I'd drink one beer when everyone else was drinking because						expected me to.
5. I'd smoke marijuana with a group of people because						expected me to.
6. I'd leave a party if people were using drugs because						expected me to.
7. I'd ignore someone who wants to be my friend because						expected me to.
8. I'd shoplift a piece of jewelry from a store because						expected me to.
9. I'd smoke a cigarette because						expected me to.
10. I'd say no to a drink because						expected me to.
11. I'd go to a church retreat because						expected me to.

Parent Track—Activity 3 Handout

What's Your Young Person's Pressure Rating?

Instructions: Below are situations in which young people feel pressured to behave certain ways. Read each situation and think about what your junior higher would do. Decide whose pressure he or she would respond to and check the appropriate boxes. Not all responses fit all situations. You may have more than one checkmark for some situations and no checkmarks for other situations.

	I	my best friend	a group of friends	my parents	God	
1. I'd wear my hair a certain way because						expected me to.
2. I'd buy a certain brand of clothing because						expected me to.
3. I'd go to a party with someone I didn't really like because						expected me to.
4. I'd drink one beer when everyone else was drinking because						expected me to.
5. I'd smoke marijuana with a group of people because						expected me to.
6. I'd leave a party if people were using drugs because						expected me to.
7. I'd ignore someone who wants to be my friend because						expected me to.
8. I'd shoplift a piece of jewelry from a store because						expected me to.
9. I'd smoke a cigarette because						expected me to.
10. I'd say no to a drink because						expected me to.
11. I'd go to a church retreat because						expected me to.

Youth and Parent Tracks
Activity 4 Handout

Scripture Cards

Scripture Card #1

Read Romans 12:2.

Discuss what you think this means in terms of how people respond to peer pressure. Think of ways people can respond to God's will and still have good relationships with their friends.

Scripture Card #2

Read Ephesians 5:18.

Discuss what you think it means to be filled with the Spirit. How does a person who's filled with the Spirit treat his or her friends? Think of ways a person filled with God's Spirit, rather than respond to pressure to drink or try drugs, can have good peer relationships.

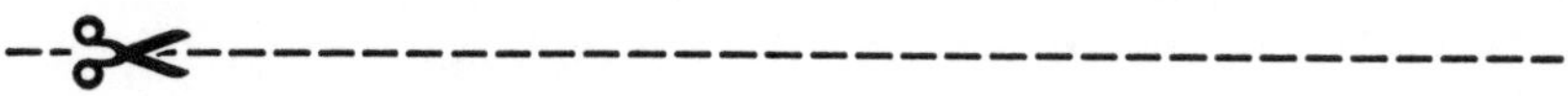

Scripture Card #3

Read Daniel 3:16-18.

Discuss what you think these three men felt when they addressed the king. Think of ways people can say no to peer pressure and still maintain good relationships with their friends.

Scripture Card #4

Read Daniel 6:10-13.

Discuss what you think Daniel felt when he disobeyed the king's command. Think of ways people can be different and still keep friends.

Youth and Parent Tracks
Activity 5 Handout

Ways to Not Give In

Instructions: The following are proven ways to not give in to people who want you to do something you don't want to do or something you know isn't right. Think about how you can use these ideas in the situations you face each day.

1. Take time to make a good decision.
2. Keep saying no.
3. Talk about something else.
4. Ignore a request that doesn't feel right.
5. Tell a funny story or joke.
6. Challenge the other person to do what he or she has asked you to do.
7. Offer an alternative.
8. Say you have to leave.
9. Find an excuse to stop talking.
10. Use your parents as an excuse.
11. Make up a reason if necessary.
12. Think of saying no as saying yes to yourself.

Youth and Parent Tracks
Activity 6 Handout

Situations

Situation #1—You and your best friend are at a party. She suggests that the two of you get some beer from the kitchen. You don't want to drink and you don't think your friend does either. What do you do?

Situation #2—A popular guy invites you to a party where you're sure there'll be lots of alcohol and drugs. You don't do that kind of stuff, but you're not sure about this guy. What do you do?

Situation #3—You're at your best friend's house. When you and your friend go into the family room, his parents offer you some pot. Your friend takes a joint. What do you do?

Situation #4—Your friend tells you she's been drinking her parents' liquor and replacing it with colored water. She asks where your parents keep their liquor. What do you do?

Situation #5—You and your best friend would like to have a party for all your friends from school. You know that many of the parties your friends go to have lots of drinking and maybe even drugs. You'd like to think of ways to have a fun party without alcohol or drugs. What do you do?

Situation #6—You're in the school parking lot before school. A person you'd like to be good friends with suggests the two of you snort some cocaine before you go inside. What do you do?

Instructions: The "At-Home Track 6" offers junior highers and parents an opportunity to discuss the issue studied in this session. Set aside 30 minutes for this meeting.

Before you begin, remember to listen as well as talk. Arguments or put-downs don't encourage conversation. Defensiveness or shouting doesn't encourage growth or change.

Now go ahead with this meeting. Follow directions and make new discoveries about yourself and other family members.

Self-esteem booster: I can say no to drugs and still have friends.

Sharing time: To begin this time together,

Parent: Talk with your young person about the "Ways to Not Give In" handout. Encourage your young person to ask questions or offer examples of how these ideas can help him or her resist drugs.

Junior higher: Talk with your parent about the alternatives poster you created. Ask your parent to support you in the alternatives you've decided on. For example, if you want to swim every day, ask your parent to take you to the pool or join you.

Bible study: Read Philippians 2:14-15 together. "Do everything without complaining or arguing, so that you may become blameless and pure, children of God without fault in a crooked and depraved generation, in which you shine like stars in the universe." Answer the following questions:

1. What does this passage say to you?

2. How can you apply this passage to your life or your family?

Activity: Take turns asking each other questions about drug use using situations such as the following:

Youth Situations

What would you do if . . .

- you're on a date with a guy or girl you like. On the way home from a movie he or she pulls out a joint and offers to share it with you.
- your group is at a friend's house after school. Suddenly, the girl who lives there comes out of the kitchen with a bottle of wine and suggests everyone pass it around. All your friends take a swallow. Now it's your turn and everyone's watching to see what you do.

• your friends look for a place to have a party and they know your parents are out of town. They call to ask if you'll have the party at your house. You know that most of the parties in your community end up being crashed by older kids who bring alcohol and drugs.

• you want to go to a dance with some of your older friends, but it's being held in a place that serves alcohol. One of your friends offers to get you a fake ID.

Parent Situations

What would you do if . . .

• your son calls you from a party and asks you to pick him up. When he gets into the car, you smell marijuana.

• you know you had two pills left in your prescription bottle. When you open the bottle, you find the pills have been replaced by a generic aspirin that looks like your prescribed pills.

• you get a phone call from your son's best friend's father. He found a syringe and white powder in his son's bedroom and the boy says they belong to your son.

• your daughter spent the night with a friend and came home sick the next morning. When she started vomiting, you became concerned and went to help her. Then you smelled the alcohol.

A plan of action: Plan a special celebration each time a family member says no to drugs. Award a special certificate, say yes to something the family member wants or needs, and talk about what happened with the rest of the family. A victory against drugs can be a learning experience for all family members.

Close this time by making a list of friends who don't pressure you to use drugs. Thank God for these friends.

SESSION 7

My Family Relationships and Drugs

Today's families are in transition. They're searching for new definitions of "family," new value systems and new functions. Throughout history, families have had clearly defined functions that have given family members a strong sense of purpose and identity. Typically families ensured economic survival, offered protection, passed on religious faith, educated their children and defined a person's status in the community according to the family name. By the 1900s most of these functions shifted to social institutions. Police and welfare agencies provide protection, schools educate children, and churches nurture religious faith. Large and small businesses and the government provide jobs that offer economic survival. And jobs measure community status for most men and women.

Since society assumes many functions of the early family, people form families today primarily to meet relational needs. People marry for intimacy and personal growth. Learning how to handle that intimacy has become a major task for modern families. Growth in the number of blended and single-parent families, more than ever before in the United States, has challenged people to redefine "family." Yet in all this transition, the majority of all Americans hold "a good family life" as a major goal for themselves.

Because one person's drug addiction can affect an entire family, it's important to understand how families function and how drug abuse can alter those patterns. This session explains the realities of life in both healthy and addicted families.

OBJECTIVES

In this session junior highers and parents will:

- identify their family's unique qualities.
- survey their family's healthy characteristics.
- talk about characteristics of healthy families and those with chemically dependent members.
- identify family roles.
- recognize and celebrate the value of Christian love within a family.

SUPPLIES

- ☐ newsprint
- ☐ markers
- ☐ masking tape
- ☐ newspapers
- ☐ construction paper
- ☐ glue
- ☐ scissors
- ☐ colored tape
- ☐ envelopes
- ☐ pencils
- ☐ adhesive bandage strips
- ☐ Bible

PREPARATION

Read the session and photocopy the handouts.

Before the meeting, write the following "Self-esteem booster" on newsprint and tape it onto the wall: "God created my family to love me. God created me to return that love and share it with others."

Set up several large tables. Place newspapers, scissors, masking tape, construction paper and glue on each table (Activity #1).

Use the colored tape to create a large circle on the floor at least 4 feet in diameter. Use six 5-foot strips of colored tape as rays radiating from the circle. Use tape to number each section created by the rays. (See diagram.)

(Activity 3)

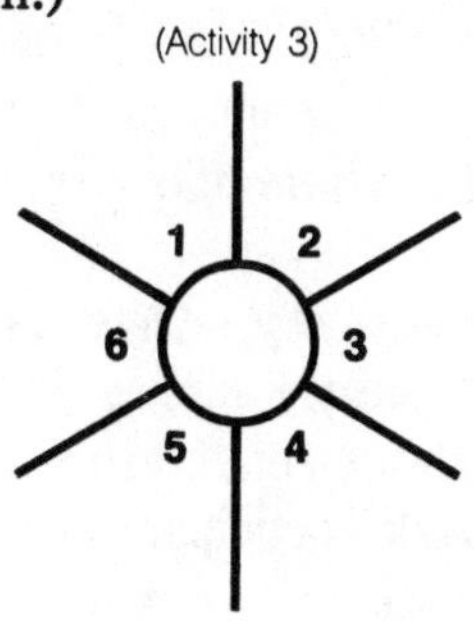

Photocopy the six "Family Sun Discussion Cards" and cut them apart. Place one card in each numbered area around the circle (Activity #3).

Make three photocopies of the "Roles of an Addicted Family" handout. For each photocopy, cut apart the roles and description clues. Place the roles in one envelope and description clues in another. You should have three sets of roles and three sets of description clues in six envelopes (Activity #4).

SESSION ACTIVITIES

1. Opening—Respond to participants' questions or comments about the last session or the "At-Home Track 6" handout.

Have participants use the items on the tables to create newspaper sculptures of their family members. Tell them they can cut, roll, wad, crush and tape the newspaper together any way they want to represent different family members. Encourage participants to make sculptures that depict unique characteristics such as interests, hobbies, strengths or activities. For example, a newspaper cut in the shape of a head with a hat may represent a father as he goes to work. Remind participants to work quickly and not spend time with details unless they finish before time's up.

When sculptures are complete, have participants place chairs in a circle. Have participants put their family sculptures in front of them. Ask participants to introduce their family members to the rest of the group along with one unique characteristic about each. For example, a young person might introduce his father sculpture by saying, "This is the person who makes our family smile a lot with his corny jokes—my dad." After participants introduce all family sculptures, have participants take their sculptures back to the tables and return to the circle of chairs.

2. Healthy families survey—Give each participant a pencil and photocopy of the "Healthy Families Survey" handout. Explain that this survey has questions related to nine different characteristics of healthy families. Ask participants to rate their families on a scale of 1 to 6 on each question (1 = never; 6 = all the time).

After participants complete their surveys and tally points for each characteristic, have them form groups of three to discuss the following questions:

- Which family characteristics are healthiest in your family (the ones with the highest number of points)?
- Which family characteristics would you like your family to improve (the ones with the lowest number of points)?
- What specific things can you do to help your family improve the characteristics you mentioned?

Encourage participants to take this handout home to show other family members during the "At-Home Track 7."

3. "Family sun" discussions—After participants discuss the questions about healthy family characteristics, ask them to arrange their chairs around the taped circle on the floor. Say: "With the newspaper sculptures and 'Healthy Families Survey' discussion, you've thought about your family members—their unique characteristics and how you operate as part of them. In this activity you'll talk more specifically about yourselves within your families.

"Look at the circle on the floor. This is our 'family sun.' The lines extending from the circle are the sun's rays. The people whose chairs fall between the rays will make a small circle with their chairs and form a discussion group. Each small group will rotate clockwise around the circle together, but leave the chairs as they rotate to a new area.

"Between the rays are numbered areas in which you have a specific discussion topic. As your group rotates, pick up the discussion card in that area and have each person take turns answering all the questions on it. At the signal, leave the card and move to the next area."

After all groups discuss the six areas, give each group a marker and newsprint. Say: "Think about what your family values most. What does your family spend most of its time doing? What's your family's most important value?" Participants' responses may include: our relationship to God and the church; work—seems like everything revolves around it; or alcohol—my mom's struggle continues to affect everything we do.

Have groups write their responses on newsprint. After a few minutes, have a volunteer from each group read the responses to the total group and place the sheet of newsprint in the center of the circle on the floor.

4. Addicted family role/description match—Say: "It's not hard to understand how a positive family environment can deter a person from experimenting with drugs. For example, young people who feel loved and supported at home are less likely to seek approval from peers whose values differ from those of their family. These young people recognize their value and seek friends who value themselves as well. These young people treat their bodies and minds with respect rather than abuse their health with drugs. When these young people approach adolescence and need to oppose their parents or question values, their healthy families can tolerate this kind of opposition. A healthy family provides a secure environment for members to talk about their ideas, questions and doubts.

"When drug abuse invades a person's life, the center of his or her family life changes. Addiction controls and influences everything the family does. Even though some addicted families believe in God, their lifestyles are characterized by reactions to the drug. Each family member typically develops a family role in response to the drug abuse. That's why drug addiction is called a family disease—everyone is affected by the addiction."

Have participants remain in their small groups. Give every other group an envelope containing roles from the "Roles of an Addicted Family" handout. Give the three remaining groups envelopes containing the description clues. Assign a group with roles and a group with clues to work together.

Ask the groups to open their envelopes and examine the contents. Have a volunteer in each description clue group read aloud the clues one at a time to the other group. The group with the roles can offer only one guess at a time after listening to each clue. When groups make a match, have a volunteer read aloud the rest of the description clues to both groups.

After all three groups complete their matches, see if there are any questions. Say: "Roles are the way some people cope with the pain of family addiction. By assuming different roles, family members take attention away from what's happening and deny there's a problem. Sometimes individuals combine several of these roles, yet the behaviors serve the same purpose—to deny pain.

"All these behaviors such as acting out, achieving, joking and withdrawing are common ways people in an addicted family cope with everyday living. These behaviors can be positive when used with flexibility and moderation; they become a problem, however, when individuals relate predominantly in these ways at the expense of dealing with deeper feelings.

"In addition to these confusing role developments, there are other symptoms of family addiction. It's important to help families recognize these symptoms and get the help they need. Listen carefully to each symptom and think of examples that illustrate this symptom."

Give participants each a photocopy of the "Symptoms of Family Addiction" handout. Read aloud each symptom and allow a few minutes for people to write examples on their handout.

If individuals have problems writing examples, offer the following examples:

1. Addicts and co-dependents continually break promises to each other and erode trust.

Because of unpredictable behavior, young people soon learn they can't count on their parents to keep their word.

When young people are addicts, their lies and cover-ups soon lead to a lack of parental trust.

2. An addict's spouse is too preoccupied with the addict's needs or struggles to consistently meet the children's emotional needs.

Because of the drug's effects, the addict either forgets or is too ashamed to affirm others.

The young addict becomes so self-centered that he or she doesn't care about others' needs.

3. The addict denies responsibility for his or her behavior while the spouse tries to rescue the addict from the natural consequences of his or her behavior.

When parents neglect their duties, the oldest child usually becomes a premature adult who learns to take care of the home and younger siblings.

Young addicts tend to blame all their problems on someone else.

4. A young person who's angry about a parent's drinking sometimes displaces his or her anger onto a brother or sister by starting arguments or treating a sibling cruelly.

An addicted parent may destroy property or abuse the spouse or children rather than deal with feelings of helplessness and anger.

A young addict's emotional outbursts may be unexpected and

uncontrolled.

5. Members of addicted families are ashamed to talk about family chaos, so they deny what's happening.

Avoiding others who might confront them with the reality of their predicament is one way family members can maintain their denial and not feel pain.

When a child becomes an addict, parents may feel totally alone and unsure about what to do so they avoid all forms of assistance.

5. The value of Christian love in the family—Say: "Striving to create a positive family environment is important for all families, especially addicted families. Sometimes looking at ourselves and how we operate at home is the first step to creating an atmosphere of love and acceptance."

Give each person a photocopy of the "Family Love Survey" handout. Ask individuals to evaluate how well they present love in their home.

After participants complete their handouts, ask them to select a partner who knows them well. Have partners talk about their responses and how realistic they are. Ask partners to discuss different family members and how these love qualities can make a difference in their lives. Remind participants to take this handout home to show their families.

6. Closing—Give each participant a marker and an adhesive bandage strip for each family member. Say: "We talked about healthy and unhealthy families and described symptoms and characteristics of both. We talked about love and how the quality of our love can make a difference in family members' lives. On the adhesive bandage strips you just received, write a love statement to each member of your family and give it to him or her when you get home. Let each family member know you'll try to keep your family healthy."

Have participants form a circle and put their arms around one another's waists. Read aloud Colossians 3:12-14. Say: "All of us are part of a family. We're also part of the larger family of God. Because of this, we inherit the support of all Christians as part of our family. When we receive love from family members, we can share that love with those around us. Let's celebrate that love with a group hug."

Distribute photocopies of the "At-Home Track 7" handout. Explain that this handout should be completed by each junior higher and his or her parent before the next session. Encourage kids or parents to schedule a time for this at-home meeting as soon as possible.

FOR SESSION 7

Youth and Parent Tracks
Activity 2 Handout

Healthy Families Survey

Instructions: Read the family characteristics and then respond to each question below by rating your family from 1 to 6 according to the following continuum.

1	2	3	4	5	6
Never	Rarely	Sometimes	Often	Most of the time	All the time

1. The family communicates openly.

_____ Do family members tell one another their thoughts and experiences regularly?

_____ Do family members express their feelings freely without fear of being punished or told they shouldn't feel that way?

_____ Do family members listen to one another?

_____ Do family members control TV time so it doesn't replace family conversations?

2. The family affirms and supports all members.

_____ Do family members express appreciation and praise for one another?

_____ Are family members accepted for who they are without feeling pressure to prove themselves by their performance?

_____ Do you feel cared about and important when you're with your family?

_____ When you make a mistake, do family members accept you anyway?

3. The family shows respect for everyone.

_____ Do family members respect one another?

_____ Are individual differences accepted by your family?

_____ Do family members treat one another's property with respect and care?

_____ Do family members treat all people as valuable?

4. The family develops trust.

_____ Do family members trust and confide in one another?

_____ Are family members truthful with one another?

_____ Can family members count on one another to be reliable and available to one another?

_____ Do family members feel peaceful and secure in their home?

continued

5. The family spends time together.

______ Do family members spend time together regularly?

______ Do family members enjoy being together?

______ Does the family play together?

______ Do family members have a sense of humor?

6. The family teaches responsibility.

______ Are family members responsible for certain chores?

______ Do family members encourage and help one another to try new responsibilities?

______ Are family members allowed to experience natural consequences when they fail to be responsible?

______ Do family members recognize responsible behavior and express appreciation for it?

7. The family shares a religious core.

______ Do family members view God as the center of their lives?

______ Does the family have a positive, hopeful approach to living?

______ Does the family attend church and pray together regularly?

______ Do family members recognize one another's imperfections and judge behavior according to intention?

8. The family shares rituals and traditions.

______ Are family stories passed down from generation to generation?

______ Are certain family traditions preserved over generations?

______ Does the family encourage a feeling of connection to the past and a link to the future family generations?

______ Does the family encourage relationships among relatives and between generations?

9. The family works at solving problems.

______ Do family members work at solving problems as soon as they arise?

______ Do family members forgive one another when there's a grievance?

______ Do family members make up after a fight?

______ Does the family seek outside help for problems it can't solve?

Tally your points for each characteristic:

1. ________ 2. ________ 3. ________ 4. ________ 5. ________

6. ________ 7. ________ 8. ________ 9. ________

Youth and Parent Tracks
Activity 3 Handout

Family Sun Discussion Cards

Respect

Who do you respect most in your family? Why?
Who don't you respect? Why?
Who respects you? Why?

Trust

Who can you always count on in your family?
Who can you tell your secrets to?
Who always keeps their promises?

Responsibility

What are your responsibilities at home?
What responsibilities do you dislike?
What responsibilities do you like?
If you fail to take care of a responsibility, what happens? Give an example.

Affirmation

Who in your family gives you hugs?
Who do you hug?
Who lets you know you're a special person? How?
What nice things do you say or do for other family members?

Communication

Who in your family do you talk to most often?
Who do you talk to about your deepest feelings?
Who do you hide your feelings from? Why?
Who seems to know how you feel before you ever talk about it?

Sharing time

Who in your family do you spend the most time with?
Who do you have the most fun with?
Who do you watch television with?
With which person would you like to go on a special vacation? What would you like to do with that person?

Youth and Parent Tracks
Activity 4 Handout

Roles of an Addicted Family

Role
the addict

Description clues
1. This person's life is controlled by a drug.
2. Using a drug comes before anything else, including responsibilities and family relationships.
3. This person's physical and psychological craving for a drug needs to be satisfied.
4. Helplessness, anger and guilt begin because this person uses so much time and energy to serve this addiction.

(Role—addict)

Role
the co-dependent or enabler

Description clues
1. This person worries about the addict's behavior and tries to control the addict's drug use.
2. This individual hides the addiction, makes excuses for unusual behavior or lies to protect the addict.
3. This individual may avoid social contact for fear of embarrassment or may become absorbed in outside activities to compensate for the loneliness of living with an addict.
4. This individual lives in constant fear of what the addict will do next.
5. When the addict promises not to use the drug again, this person wants to believe. But he or she watches the addict break promises again and again and finally loses all hope.

(Role—co-dependent or enabler)

Role
the scapegoat

Description clues
1. Usually a child in the family, this individual gets into trouble and provides an opportunity for family members to shift their anger from the addict to the "troublemaker."
2. This individual feels lonely and sacrifices self for attention.

(Role—scapegoat)

continued

Role
the superkid

Description clues
1. This individual is a high-achiever and a leader among peers.
2. Often the oldest child, this person has learned leadership by taking responsibility for younger siblings and neglected housework.
3. This kid provides success for the family.
4. This individual is usually praised by teachers and neighbors who mistakenly believe that this child must come from a perfect home.
(Role—superkid)

Role
the clown

Description clues
1. This individual learns to make jokes and create distractions.
2. Attempts at humor are aimed at relieving family tension and pain.
(Role—clown)

Role
the withdrawn child

Description clues
1. This young person learns helplessness and hiding to cope with family chaos and pain.
2. This person typically gets involved in individual activity in an isolated room or remains as quiet as possible.
(Role—withdrawn child)

Youth and Parent Tracks
Activity 4 Handout

Symptoms of Family Addiction

Instructions: Read each symptom and write examples in the space below each symptom.

The family foundation of trust is broken.

Emotional support and the ability to affirm one another disappear.

Responsibility for behavior is distorted and confused.

Expression of feelings may be indirect or inappropriate.

Families typically feel isolated even within their community of neighbors and friends.

Instructions: Read the following scripture passage. Then read "Love's Qualities" and rate yourself from 1 to 10 on how much you share that quality of love with your family (1 = never; 10 = always).

"Love is patient, love is kind. It does not envy, it does not boast, it is not proud. It is not rude, it is not self-seeking, it is not easily angered, it keeps no record of wrongs. Love does not delight in evil but rejoices with the truth. It always protects, always trusts, always hopes, always perseveres" (1 Corinthians 13:4-7).

Love's Qualities

LOVE is patient.

I'm patient with family members. I listen carefully to what they say and seek to understand their motives for what they do. I rarely get angry and I never yell.

1	2	3	4	5	6	7	8	9	10
Never									Always

LOVE is kind.

I'm thoughtful and caring toward family members. I try to support and encourage family members. When others do special things for me, I let them know I appreciate their efforts.

1	2	3	4	5	6	7	8	9	10
Never									Always

LOVE doesn't envy.

I don't get upset when someone else in the family gets something and I don't. I don't get angry when another family member succeeds and I don't. I don't keep track of who gets what or demand my equal share.

1	2	3	4	5	6	7	8	9	10
Never									Always

LOVE doesn't boast.

I don't try to be the most important person in my family. I don't want extra attention nor do I expect special treatment. I work to help all my family members feel important.

1	2	3	4	5	6	7	8	9	10
Never									Always

LOVE isn't proud.

I try to understand my limitations. I don't let my ego determine how I act toward or react to family members. I don't put others down when they don't meet my expectations.

1	2	3	4	5	6	7	8	9	10
Never									Always

continued

LOVE isn't rude.

I don't use sarcasm and biting comments with my family. I don't deliberately hurt family members with my language or actions. I try to support family members in all that I do.

1 Never	2	3	4	5	6	7	8	9	10 Always

LOVE isn't self-seeking.

I don't try to make the family conform to my way of doing things. I don't make demands of other family members just to make my life easier.

1 Never	2	3	4	5	6	7	8	9	10 Always

LOVE isn't easily angered.

I'm not supersensitive, so my family members don't have to be afraid of offending me. I don't intentionally irritate other family members. I try to be easygoing with my family.

1 Never	2	3	4	5	6	7	8	9	10 Always

LOVE doesn't remember wrongs.

I've learned how important forgiveness is in my family. I forgive freely and don't hold grudges. I don't belittle other family members because of their mistakes.

1 Never	2	3	4	5	6	7	8	9	10 Always

LOVE rejoices in truth, not evil.

I don't delight in another family member's failure, even when it makes me look good. When facing tough family times, I try to encourage other family members, not put them down.

1 Never	2	3	4	5	6	7	8	9	10 Always

LOVE always perseveres.

When I'm angry with a family member, I never give up on our relationship. I know we can work out our difficulties. I keep talking and let that person know I care regardless of how that family member treats me.

1 Never	2	3	4	5	6	7	8	9	10 Always

Instructions: The "At-Home Track 7" offers junior highers and parents an opportunity to discuss the issue studied in this session. Set aside 30 minutes for this meeting.

Before you begin, remember to listen as well as talk. Arguments or put-downs don't encourage conversation. Defensiveness or shouting doesn't encourage growth or change.

Now go ahead with this meeting. Follow directions and make new discoveries about yourself and other family members.

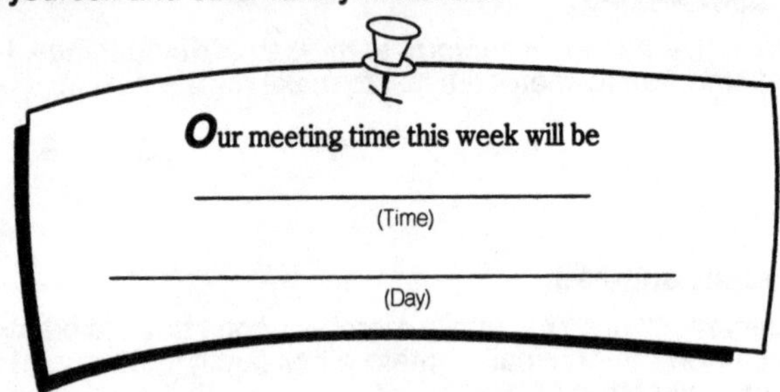

Self-esteem booster: God created my family to love me. God created me to return that love and share it with others.

Sharing time: To begin this time together,

Parent and junior higher: Review characteristics of healthy families on the "Healthy Families Survey" you took in this session. Talk about the ideas you had for improving some of these characteristics in your home. Discuss the "Family Love Survey" you completed for your family.

Bible study: Read Ephesians 5:1-2, 15-21 together. "Be imitators of God, therefore, as dearly loved children and live a life of love, just as Christ loved us and gave himself up for us as a fragrant offering and sacrifice to God . . . Be very careful, then, how you live—not as unwise but as wise, making the most of every opportunity, because the days are evil. Therefore do not be foolish, but understand what the Lord's will is. Do not get drunk on wine, which leads to debauchery. Instead, be filled with the Spirit. Speak to one another with psalms, hymns and spiritual songs. Sing and make music in your heart to the Lord, always giving thanks to God the Father for everything, in the name of our Lord Jesus Christ." Answer the following questions:

1. What does this passage say to you?

2. How can you apply this passage to your life or your family?

continued

Activity: Look around your house for props that symbolize each person's role in your family. For example, you might choose a big, warm coat to symbolize your dad who offers warmth to the family. Or you might choose a hymnal to symbolize a daughter as the musical director of your family. Be creative.

Bring all your props together and talk about why you chose each one.

A plan of action: Plan a family celebration before the next session. Decide when and where it'll be and what you'll do. For example, you could have a game night when each person thinks of a game to play. Or you could organize a family picnic with each family member responsible for planning and carrying out the celebration.

Close this time together by planning the family celebration.

Our celebration:

Date:

Time:

Place:

Responsibilities:

SESSION 8

I'm Part of a Solution!

Drugs, God & Me examines ways to help young people avoid drug abuse or deal with those who have chosen that option. Positive self-esteem, communication skills, healthy ways of handling feelings, knowledge of drugs and their effects, decision-making skills, ways to say no, healthy family life, supportive relationships and Christian faith—all these factors combine to create happy and healthy lifestyles. Rather than focus on the use or misuse of drugs, this session concentrates on helping individuals make healthy decisions dedicated to bringing wholeness to life.

Preventing drug abuse doesn't stop with the individual. Drug abuse does threaten a person's emotional, spiritual, intellectual and physical well-being. But it also threatens that person's family, friends, church, school, work place and community. Drug-related problems affect everyone to varying degrees. This session encourages participants to reach out and become part of a solution to the drug abuse problem.

OBJECTIVES

In this session junior highers and parents will:

• become involved in an activity that demonstrates the importance of working together to find a solution to a problem.

• complete a health assessment inventory.

• listen to a scripture passage and write a parable that illustrates what this scripture says about responding to people in trouble with drugs.

• discuss symptoms of drug abuse and how to respond.

• brainstorm ideas for preventing drug abuse in the church,

schools and community.

• develop an individual plan of action for being part of a solution to drug abuse.

SUPPLIES

- ☐ newsprint
- ☐ markers
- ☐ masking tape
- ☐ envelopes
- ☐ stamps
- ☐ paper
- ☐ pencils
- ☐ package of wheat crackers
- ☐ package of individually wrapped chocolates
- ☐ large basket
- ☐ Bible

PREPARATION

Read the session and photocopy the handouts.

Before the meeting, write the following "Self-esteem booster" on newsprint and tape it onto the wall: "I can be part of a solution to drug abuse."

Tape a blank sheet of newsprint onto the wall. Draw a line from top to bottom making two columns. Label one column "Wheat Crackers" and the other column "Chocolate Candy" (Activity #2).

Gather information about community resources available for drug-related problems (Activity #4). Invite a professional drug abuse counselor to attend this session to answer participants' questions (Activity #4). Mark the calendar and put stamps on envelopes to mail participants' "My Action Plan" handouts to them 30 days after this session (Activity #6).

SESSION ACTIVITIES

1. Opening—Respond to participants' questions or comments about the last session or the "At-Home Track 7" handout.

Have participants form circles of five to seven people. Give the groups the following instructions:

• Reach across your circle and join hands with two different people in your group. Crisscross your arms above and below the arms of other people.

• At the signal, unravel the tangled mass of arms. Hands should remain joined at all times. You'll step over arms and crawl under legs to unravel this human knot.

• The goal is to unravel the knot to form a circle of people still holding hands, even though some people face in and some face out.

After completing this activity, point out the "Self-esteem booster" taped to the wall and say: "We just completed an activity that demonstrates how working together on a problem helps us find a solution. In this last session, we'll talk about how we can work together to be part of a solution to the drug abuse problem."

2. A chemical health assessment—Have participants form a circle with their chairs. Pass a package of wheat crackers and a package of individually wrapped chocolates around the circle, inviting individuals to choose. After both packages have made a complete circle, encourage people to eat their choice. Then say: "The first way we can be part of a solution to drug abuse is to live a healthy lifestyle. Think about the crackers and candy I passed around the circle. Which item do you like best? Which is best for you? Which did you select? Should you be able to eat both? Which would bother you most if you overindulged?"

After participants acknowledge that candy is the less healthy choice, say, "In the 'Wheat Crackers' column let's list activities that promote health and wellness." Suggestions might include jogging, eating nutritious food or hugging family members.

After you list at least 10 items, say, "In the 'Chocolate Candy' column let's list things that are unhealthy and can lead to serious problems." Suggestions might include refusing to express any feelings when we're angry, watching excessive amounts of television, making frequent stops at the ice cream store or smoking cigarettes. List at least 10 items in this column also. Ask: "Can you think of any other ideas to add to these lists? What makes these choices healthy or unhealthy?"

After a brief discussion, give each person a pencil and photocopy of the "Chemical Health Assessment" handout. Read aloud the instructions and assure participants no one will examine their answers.

After participants complete their "Chemical Health Assessment" handout, inform them that circling one Yes indicates danger, two Yeses indicates a strong possibility of trouble and three Yeses designates a clear problem. Encourage participants who answered Yes to any of these questions to seek help by talking to someone. Suggest a parent, trusted adult or professional counselor. Remind individuals they can be part of a solution by getting help if there's a problem.

3. A modern-day parable—Have participants form groups of four. Give a sheet of paper to each small group. Read aloud Luke 10:25-37. Say: "In this familiar story, the man was almost destroyed by robbers who left him half-dead. Today, many people are being destroyed by drugs that lead them toward death. In your small groups write a modern-day parable about how to help a friend in trouble with drugs. For example, you might write about receiving a phone call from a friend who's drunk and threatening to take his or her life."

After the small groups finish, have a volunteer from each group read aloud the parable. Ask participants how they would respond in each situation.

4. Knowing how to help others—Say: "The second way we can be part of a solution to drug abuse is to help others who have drug-related problems. To do this we need to know the signs of drug abuse and how to respond to them."

Give each person photocopies of the "Warning Signals of Drug Abuse" and "How to Deal With a Drug Abuser" handouts. Say: "It's important to know how to recognize drug abuse symptoms so you can encourage friends who display these symptoms to get help. Sometimes a confrontation with a close friend can do more to get that person to get help than numerous lectures and piles of information."

Read these handouts with the group. Encourage questions and discussion. If you can't answer a question, make a note and call a professional for the answer—or you might ask a professional drug abuse counselor to attend this final session. Give participants current information about community resources available for drug-related problems such as the local Alcoholics Anonymous, Al-Anon and Alateen groups.

5. Reaching out—Say: "The third way we can be part of a solution to drug abuse is to work in the church, schools and community toward preventing drug abuse. Let's brainstorm ways to prevent drug abuse through our church, schools and community."

Have participants form groups of five. Give each small group newsprint and a marker. Have group members write ideas on newsprint to discuss in the total group. Give small groups 15 minutes to complete this activity.

While participants brainstorm, tape a large sheet of newsprint horizontally onto the wall. Divide it into three parts labeled "Church," "School" and "Community."

Youth Track

Some prevention ideas young people might suggest:

Church

1. Organize a kids support group.
2. Provide junior high mentors for younger kids to talk to about drugs or other problems.

School

1. Establish a "Just Say No!" club.
2. Organize alternative (drug-free) parties.

Community

1. Encourage friends to participate in community activities that promote getting high without drugs.
2. Talk to friends about help that's available in the community.

Parent Track

Some prevention ideas parents might suggest:

Church

1. Set up an educational series on alcohol and drugs.
2. Organize a parents support group.

School

1. Volunteer as an adult sponsor at school activities to get to know the kids.
2. Befriend young people who need support and encouragement.

Community

1. Volunteer to help with activities that promote natural highs for young people such as the 4-H, sports teams or hiking groups.
2. Encourage businesses and professional organizations to present motivational opportunities for young people such as seminars for young entrepreneurs. Have them encourage kids to get their highs from something besides drugs.

Have each small group share its ideas with the total group. Record ideas on the large sheet of newsprint. Encourage participants to ask questions or discuss ideas they don't understand.

6. My action plan—Give each person an envelope and a photocopy of the "My Action Plan" handout. Ask participants to fill out the plan as part of their commitment to be part of a solution. Tell them to use any ideas listed during the brainstorming session or create their own. Encourage them to write specific goals such as "I'll make an appointment with the school counselor Tuesday to talk about organizing a 'Just Say No!' club." Have participants fold their "My Action Plan" handouts, put them in envelopes, and write their names and home addresses on the front. When most people are finished, pass a basket to collect the envelopes. Let people know they'll receive their plans in the mail in about a month as a reminder to continue to be part of a solution.

Ask participants to meet with a partner and share one of their goals or changes. Have partners pray for each other and the success of their efforts.

7. Evaluation—Give individuals a photocopy of the appropriate evaluation form for *Drugs, God & Me*. Ask them to complete the form and be as specific as possible.

8. Closing—Collect evaluations and have participants form a circle. Give each person a photocopy of the "I'm Part of a Solution!" handout and ask them to read responsively.

Thank everyone for participating in the course. Remind them they have a support group in the people who attended this course with them. Encourage them to keep in touch as they strive to be part of a solution to drug abuse.

Hand out photocopies of the "At-Home Track 8" handout. Encourage participants to use this handout to have family time and maintain the opportunity to talk.

Youth and Parent Tracks
Activity 2 Handout

Chemical Health Assessment

Instructions: Read each question and circle the correct response. Answer questions honestly. This assessment is designed to help you decide whether you're in danger or have a drug problem.

Yes No 1. Do you lose time from school/work due to drug use or alcohol consumption?

Yes No 2. Do you drink or take drugs because you're shy?

Yes No 3. Do you drink or use drugs to build your self-confidence?

Yes No 4. Do you drink or take drugs alone?

Yes No 5. Is your drinking or drug-taking affecting your reputation?

Yes No 6. Do you drink or use drugs to escape responsibilities or worries?

Yes No 7. Do you feel guilty after drinking or using drugs?

Yes No 8. Does it bother you if someone says you drink too much or have no business taking drugs?

Yes No 9. Do you feel you must use alcohol or drugs to relax when you're with a person of the opposite sex?

Yes No 10. Have you experienced financial difficulty due to buying alcohol or drugs?

Yes No 11. Do you feel a sense of power when you drink or use drugs?

Yes No 12. Have you begun to associate with a crowd that has alcohol or drugs readily available?

Yes No 13. Have you lost friends or destroyed a relationship since you've started using alcohol or drugs more frequently?

Yes No 14. Do your friends drink less alcohol than you do?

Yes No 15. Do you drink alcohol until the bottle is empty?

Yes No 16. Have you ever had a complete loss of memory from drinking?

Yes No 17. Have you ever been admitted to a hospital or arrested due to drinking or drug use?

Yes No 18. Do you ignore or dismiss studies or lectures about drinking or drug abuse?

Yes No 19. Do your family members or friends think you have a problem with drinking or drugs?

Yes No 20. Do you think you have a problem with drinking or drugs?

Youth and Parent Tracks
Activity 4 Handout

Warning Signals of Drug Abuse

Instructions: Read these signals and familiarize yourself with them.

Drug abuse is a powerful form of self-destruction. Major drug abuse symptoms include:

1. regular use of a drug.

2. personality changes and mood swings.

3. irresponsible behavior such as missing school/work or failing to do homework/the job.

4. loss of interest in outside activities, especially recreational or creative activities.

5. a change in friends to a group that supports drug use.

6. dwindling financial resources that are spent on drugs.

7. concern expressed by neighbors or friends about the user's behavior.

8. trouble with the law such as arrests for assault or driving under the influence of drugs.

9. strong, negative reactions to comments about his or her drug use.

10. refusal to listen to someone from Alcoholics Anonymous or talks about drug abuse.

11. fighting or vandalism.

12. medical problems such as gastritis, ulcers or injuries from accidents.

13. lying, manipulating or stealing.

14. hiding drugs or paraphernalia such as pipes, spoons, papers or needles.

15. outward physical signs such as alcohol on the breath, hyperactivity or sluggishness.

16. isolation from family and friends.

17. withdrawal from school and community activities.

18. impaired relationships with important people in the user's life.

Youth and Parent Tracks
Activity 4 Handout

How to Deal With a Drug Abuser

Instructions: Read these guidelines and familiarize yourself with them. If you recognize drug abuse symptoms, remember one person alone can't stop an abuser. Recruiting professional guidance is essential.

When responding to a drug abuser, some dos and don'ts include the following:

1. Don't accept any lies.

2. Don't let the abuser manipulate you into feeling guilty for his or her problem.

3. Don't lecture, praise, blame or provoke the abuser.

4. Don't cover up drug abuse consequences for the abuser.

5. Don't accept the abuser's promises that he or she will do things differently next time.

6. Don't threaten. If you do, be prepared to carry out your threat to the fullest.

7. Do get others involved in efforts to help the abuser.

8. Do propose and offer alternatives for getting high without drugs.

Youth and Parent Tracks
Activity 6 Handout

My  Plan

I can be part of a solution to drug abuse by:

1. **adopting a healthy, chemical-free lifestyle.**
2. **helping friends who abuse drugs get help.**
3. **reaching out in the church, schools and community to prevent drug abuse.**

I'll set the following goals or make the following changes to carry out this action plan:

1.

2.

3.

4.

5.

Signed:______________________________

Date:______________________________

Youth Track—Activity 7 Handout

Youth Evaluation of Drugs, God & Me

Instructions: Complete the following open-ended statements. Your ideas will help improve this course and provide insight into what additional information is needed.

1. The most valuable thing I gained from this course is ____.

2. The information I want to share with my best friend is ____.

3. The information I want to talk about with my parents is ____.

4. What I enjoyed most about this course was ____.

5. This course could be improved by ____.

6. As a result of this course, a change I've made is ____.

7. Questions about drug abuse I still have are ____.

8. Other comments or suggestions: ____.

Signature ______________________
(optional)

Parent Track—Activity 7 Handout

Parent Evaluation of Drugs, God & Me

Instructions: Complete the following open-ended statements. Your ideas will help improve this course and provide insight into what additional information is needed.

1. The most valuable thing I gained from this course is ______________________________.

2. The information I want to share with friends and other parents is ______________________________.

3. The information I want to talk about with my young person is ______________________________.

4. What I enjoyed most about this course was ______________________________.

5. This course could be improved by ______________________________.

6. As a result of this course, a change I've made is ______________________________.

7. Questions about drug abuse I still have are ______________________________.

8. Other comments or suggestions: ______________________________.

Signature ______________________________
(optional)

Youth and Parent Tracks
Activity 8 Handout

I'm Part of a Solution!

Leader: God, you've made each of us special and unique.

All: Thanks, God!

Leader: You've given each of us deep feelings and you've been with us when we need to deal with them.

All: Thanks, God!

Leader: You've given us the opportunity to care for your creations.

All: Thanks, God!

Leader: You've given us wonderful bodies to use for your glory.

All: Thanks, God!

Leader: You've given us the intelligence to make healthy decisions regarding drugs.

All: Thanks, God!

Leader: You've provided us with ways to say no to drugs and still maintain our friendships.

All: Thanks, God!

Leader: You've created families to give us love and given us reasons to return that love, extending that love to others outside our families.

All: Thanks, God!

Leader: You've given us awareness, understanding and an ability to think how we can help friends and family members avoid drug abuse.

All: Thanks, God, for using us as part of a solution! Amen.

Instructions: The "At-Home Track 8" offers junior highers and parents an opportunity to discuss the issue studied in this session. Set aside 30 minutes for this meeting.

Before you begin, remember to listen as well as talk. Arguments or put-downs don't encourage conversation. Defensiveness or shouting doesn't encourage growth or change.

Now go ahead with this meeting. Follow directions and make new discoveries about yourself and other family members.

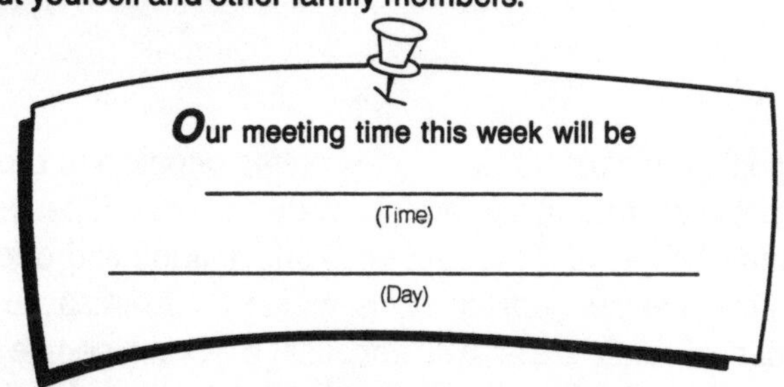

Self-esteem booster: I can be part of a solution to drug abuse.

Sharing time: To begin this time together,

Parent and junior higher: Talk about the course, *Drugs, God & Me*, what you learned, what you don't understand, how you feel about drugs and how you can be part of a solution. Listen to each other.

Bible study: Read 1 Corinthians 13:8-13 together. "Love never fails. But where there are prophecies, they will cease; where there are tongues, they will be stilled; where there is knowledge, it will pass away. For we know in part and we prophesy in part, but when perfection comes, the imperfect disappears. When I was a child, I talked like a child, I thought like a child, I reasoned like a child. When I became a man, I put childish ways behind me. Now we see but a poor reflection as in a mirror; then we shall see face to face. Now I know in part; then I shall know fully, even as I am fully known. And now these three remain: faith, hope and love. But the greatest of these is love." Answer the following questions:

1. What does this passage say to you?
2. How can you apply this passage to your life or your family?

Activity: Continue meeting once a week for the next six weeks to discuss the following topics:

- Our family: What I like and what I'd like to change.
- Family celebrations: How we can have highs without drugs.
- Stress in the family: How we can help one another make good decisions for alternatives to drug use.
- My friends and the family: How we can help one another's friends feel welcome and accepted in our home.
- Making mistakes: What I can expect from family members when I do something wrong.
- Questions I still have about drug abuse.

A plan of action: Schedule a meeting six weeks away to talk about the "My Action Plan" handouts you completed during Session 8. Offer congratulations for those goals accomplished. Provide support and encouragement for the goals you're still working toward.

Remember to pray with and for one another as you struggle with drug abuse problems. Opening lines of communication and offering love create a positive family environment in which family members can relate and grow. Remember you *are* a part of the solution!

Retreat for Youth and Parents

The goal of this retreat is to offer young people and their parents tools to prevent drug abuse among young people. The retreat provides young people and parents with information and opportunities to build personal relationship skills within a Christian perspective. The leader of each track will encourage young people and their parents to grow in their understanding of one another and themselves.

Objectives

During this retreat participants will:

- discuss ways to develop self-esteem.
- talk about ways to deal with feelings.
- acknowledge themselves as caretakers of God's creations.
- seek ways to glorify God with their bodies.
- recognize and practice responsibility for making good decisions.
- learn how to say no and maintain friendships.
- acknowledge the value of love in creating a positive family atmosphere.
- plan how individuals can be part of a solution to drug abuse.

Preparation

Supplies you'll need (in addition to those for each session):

☐ balloons
☐ popcorn poppers, popcorn, salt and oil
☐ two baskets
☐ a long, heavy tug-of-war rope
☐ a bandanna

☐ free-time supplies such as bandannas to tie legs together for the three-legged race, or a volleyball set
☐ celebration games or activities such as bingo or Pictionary
☐ a fun video such as a Disney movie or musical
☐ nutritious snacks such as fruit, cheese, crackers, peanut butter, apple cider, granola bars, fruit juice, homemade oatmeal cookies and lemonade
☐ individually wrapped chocolates
☐ pop and candy bars
☐ food for meals

Before the retreat—Recruit two or more adults to aid you in retreat planning. These people can help with programming, logistics, transportation or other needs.

Photocopy the handouts for all sessions. Read all the sessions and complete all preparations before the retreat.

Retreat Schedule

Friday

6:30 p.m.	Arrive and unpack
7 p.m.	Group singing
7:15 p.m.	Overdoser
7:30 p.m.	Session 1
8:30 p.m.	Break for a healthy snack
9 p.m.	Session 2
10 p.m.	Filling everyone's shoes
11 p.m.	Prepare for bed
11:30 p.m.	Lights out

Saturday

7 a.m.	Wake-up call
8 a.m.	Breakfast
8:45 a.m.	Devotions
9 a.m.	Session 3
10 a.m.	Stretch to refresh yourself
10:30 a.m.	Session 4
11:30 a.m.	Take a family walk
Noon	Lunch
1 p.m.	Free time
2:30 p.m.	Session 5

3:30 p.m.	Make a healthy choice
4:30 p.m.	Session 6
5:30 p.m.	Dinner
6:30 p.m.	The power hour
7:30 p.m.	Session 7
8:30 p.m.	Celebration
9:30 p.m.	Popcorn party
10 p.m.	Relaxing activity
11 p.m.	Prepare for bed
11:30 p.m.	Lights out

Sunday

7 a.m.	Wake-up call
8 a.m.	Breakfast
8:45 a.m.	Devotions
9 a.m.	Session 8
10 a.m.	Closing worship
11 a.m.	Pack
11:30 a.m.	Lunch
12:30 p.m.	Leave for home

Retreat
Friday

Overdoser—Have participants stand in a circle in the center of the room. Say: "After I give these instructions, I'll ask everyone to close his or her eyes while I walk around the circle. When I circle the group, I'll secretly touch someone on the back and that person will be the 'overdoser.' The overdoser's goal is to kill all the group members by winking at them one at a time before anyone discovers who the overdoser is. Only the overdoser can wink at people.

"When the game begins, people should open their eyes and mill around the room looking other people in the eye. The overdoser should mill around with the others. Approximately every 30 seconds, he or she will isolate an individual and wink at that person to give him or her a lethal overdose. When you're winked at, you must die by falling to the floor or sitting where you are. Victims can be melodramatic if they want but should try not to reveal the overdoser's identity.

"The object of this game is to identify the overdoser. As soon as you think you can identify the overdoser, stand still and raise a hand. When I see two people with hands raised, I'll call out, 'Stop!' All individuals should freeze where they are.

"I'll ask the two people with their hands up to simultaneously point to the overdoser. If they point to two different people, both the accusers must fall down and die from an overdose. If they point to the same person who isn't the overdoser, the accusers must also fall down as victims of an overdose. If they point to the same person who's the correct overdoser, the game is over. If they don't identify the correct overdoser, I'll ask you to mill around until the overdoser is correctly identified."

Begin the game. If people identify the overdoser right away, play another round by starting over with the circle.

Session 1—(See page 12.)

Break for a healthy snack—Offer fruit, cheese and crackers. Foods such as these emphasize the importance of taking care of our bodies through nutrition.

Session 2—(See page 24.)

Filling everyone's shoes—Have participants form two or more circles, mixing parents and young people. Explain that when you give the signal, individuals should take off their shoes and pass them to the person on their right. Explain that individuals must put on both shoes (they don't have to tie or buckle them). They must stand and turn around six times. Then they must sit, take them off and pass them to the next person on the right.

When each person gets his or her own shoes, he or she has to put them on, tie or buckle them and then stand. Announce that the group that finishes first will be first in line for breakfast.

Because of different shoe sizes, some people won't be able to put on the other contestants' shoes. If individuals get shoes that are too small, they must get their feet in as far as possible so they can stand and turn around. Because wearing small shoes doesn't help a person's balance, there'll be lots of laughable tumbles.

Remind group members that when we try to walk in another person's shoes, sometimes they don't fit. It's important to allow each person to walk in his or her own shoes and celebrate each person's unique qualities.

Ask family groups to meet together to talk about the unique qualities family members appreciate about one another. As families finish their discussions, individuals can get ready for bed.

Saturday

Devotions—Have family groups sit together. Ask a volunteer to read aloud 1 Corinthians 12:14-27. Instruct family members to take turns telling one another which human body part represents each person in their family. For example, someone might think of their mother as the heart because she's loving and "pumps" people up when they're down.

After family members finish talking, close with a prayer that recognizes each family member's unique value. Pray that God will help each person look beyond the family to celebrate the unique value of others outside the family.

Session 3—(See page 46.)

Stretch to refresh yourself—Ask the more energetic participants to lead the group in stretching exercises. Serve a nutritious snack such as peanut butter and apples, or apple cider and granola bars.

Session 4—(See page 65.)

Take a family walk—Encourage families to take a Bible and spend time walking and talking together about what they've experienced so far. After discussing their responsibilities to God's creations and realizing that the human body is one of God's greatest creations, participants should read Ephesians 2:10. Then family members can discuss how each can be the best representative of "God's workmanship."

Lunch

Free time—Junior highers are normally active and energetic, way beyond most parents' energy level. Schedule relays such as a three-legged race to include young people with their parents, but intersperse activities for junior highers only. For example, you could schedule a volleyball tournament. Have the junior highers form three groups. Schedule two junior high teams to play each other, with the winner playing the third junior high team. Then the winner of the second game could play the parents. This kind of scheduling allows parents time to rest and offers opportunities for the young people to expend their energy. Make activities optional since some people may choose this time to read or rest.

Session 5—(See page 80.)

Make a healthy choice—Give participants a choice of snacks. Have pop and candy bars at one end of a table and fruit juice and homemade oatmeal cookies at the other end. Place a sign, "Make a Healthy Choice," in the center of the table. Not all people will make a healthy choice, but you'll have made your point.

Session 6—(See page 98.)

Dinner

The power hour—Tie a bandanna in the center of a long, heavy rope. Lay the rope in a straight line on the ground outside your meeting place. Draw two lines five feet to either side of the bandanna.

Have all participants join you outside. Ask the parents to go to one end of the rope and kids to the other end. Say: "Tonight we're going to have a power struggle between parents and kids. When I give the signal, pick up your end of the rope and get ready to pull. The team that pulls the bandanna across the line on its side wins the first round. There'll be three pulls. The team that wins two out of three pulls wins the power struggle."

When a winner has been declared, have both teams sit and talk about how a tug of war is like the power struggle that occurs between parents and young people. Point out that both parents and young people have power; therefore, it's important to learn how to use that power for good.

Ask parents to form a circle. Have the junior highers form another circle around their parents. Explain that parents and kids will discuss the same questions separately. Encourage participants to speak as generally as possible so as not to point the finger at their own family members. Since parents will have their discussion first, encourage kids to listen and learn from the opinions their parents express. Let the kids know they'll discuss the same questions and parents will have to listen. Ask parents the following questions:

- What kind of power do kids have in the parent-child relationship?
- What kind of power do parents have in the parent-child relationship?
- How can kids abuse their power?
- How can kids use their power wisely?
- How can parents abuse their power?
- How can parents use their power wisely?

When parents complete their discussion, ask the junior highers to form a circle and have parents form a circle around them. Repeat the instructions for people inside and outside the circle. Then ask the kids to discuss the same questions their parents discussed.

Close "The power hour" by asking family groups to meet together. Have each family member talk about one way he or she will use his or her power wisely.

Session 7—(See page 116.)

Celebration—Ask family groups to meet together. Give each family magazines, construction paper, glue, masking tape, scissors, markers and a balloon for each family member. Instruct family groups to inflate their balloons and designate each one a particular family member. Have family members cut out pictures, write words, make symbols or decorate the balloons in different ways to indicate each family member's healthy characteristics. When decorating is complete, have each family member use the balloons to explain to other family members how they help make the home a pleasant, loving environment.

After family groups finish talking, have them use their balloons and make other items to decorate the room for the "Popcorn party." They might make paper chains or create posters about what makes a healthy family.

Popcorn party—Ask participants to form four groups. Have one group prepare the popcorn and another group prepare drinks such as lemonade or fruit juice. Ask the third group to set up the games or activities such as bingo, Pictionary or charades. Have the fourth group set up the videocassette recorder and TV set for the video shown during the "Relaxing activity." After preparations are complete, have participants get their refreshments and begin the games.

Relaxing activity—Play a fun video such as a Disney movie, musical or family movie that participants will enjoy.

Sunday

Devotions—Ask participants to form family groups. Have a volunteer read aloud 1 John 4:7-12. Ask family groups to discuss the following questions:

- What difference does it make in our family that love comes from God?
- How is God's love evident in our home?
- How can we share God's love with others outside our home?

After families have discussed these questions, have each family member say to every other family member, "I see the evidence of God's love in you by . . ." Close the devotions with a prayer that God will help each person use his or her godlike qualities to reach out to others in their struggle against drug abuse.

Session 8—(See page 134.) Ask participants to take their "My Action Plan" handouts to the "Closing worship" instead of collecting them during the session.

Closing worship—Have a volunteer read aloud Psalm 139:1-4. Ask family members to sit together and talk about one goal they have from their action plan in the last session.

Have a volunteer read aloud Psalm 139:13-18. Have family members talk about what it means to them that God knows them so intimately. Encourage them to discuss how knowing God makes a difference in their lives.

Have a volunteer read aloud Psalm 139:23-24. Place two baskets in the center of the room, one empty and one filled with individually wrapped chocolates. Ask each family to bring its action plans from the last session to the empty basket and take a chocolate from the other basket. Have families make one large circle around the two baskets.

Say: "These candies could be considered drugs because chocolate contains caffeine. These candies remind us that every day we have the power to make wise or foolish choices about whether to use drugs. What you do with this candy is your choice. You may choose to unwrap the candy as a symbol to open yourself to friends. Or you may eat the candy, acknowledging that chocolate is a safe drug, used in moderation. Keep the wrapper as a reminder of your commitment to make wise choices about using drugs. Think about how this candy can be a symbol for the choice you want to make about drugs. Tell your thought to one of the people next to you." Make sure everyone has someone to talk to.

Ask participants to put their arms around the people on either side of them as a symbol of support. Close the meeting with a prayer that God will help each person as he or she struggles with drug abuse. Thank God for his gifts of power and love, especially as they're expressed through others.

Retreat for Kids

The goal of this retreat is to provide junior highers with tools to resist drug abuse. This retreat provides kids with information and opportunities for building personal relationship skills within a Christian perspective. Young people will be encouraged to take home what they learn to discuss this issue with their parents.

Objectives

During this retreat junior highers will:

- experience activities that help develop self-esteem.
- talk about ways to deal with their feelings.
- acknowledge themselves as caretakers of God's creations.
- seek ways to glorify God with their bodies.
- discuss how to make good decisions and practice the steps.
- learn how to say no and maintain friendships.
- discuss the value of love in the family and how they can help create a positive family atmosphere.
- plan how they can be part of a solution to drug abuse.

Preparation

Supplies you'll need (in addition to those for each session):

- ☐ balloons
- ☐ string
- ☐ popcorn poppers, popcorn, salt and oil
- ☐ free-time supplies such as volleyball and croquet sets
- ☐ a fun video such as a Disney movie or musical
- ☐ pop and candy bars
- ☐ one large bottle of cola with caffeine
- ☐ a variety of jackets, hats and gloves for the "Clothing scramble"
- ☐ one-pound coffee cans
- ☐ nutritious snacks such as fruit, peanut butter, cheese spread,

lemonade, fruit juice, granola bars, cut raw vegetables and yogurt dip

- ☐ items for fitness stations such as jump ropes, timers and tape measures
- ☐ food for meals
- ☐ songbooks

Before the retreat—Recruit two or more adults to aid you in planning. These people can help with programming, logistics, transportation and other needs. Find adult volunteers to accompany you on the retreat. Aim for one adult for every six junior highers.

Photocopy the handouts for all "Youth Track" sessions. Read all the "Youth Track" sessions and complete all preparations before the retreat.

Write instructions for the fitness stations on 3×5 cards. Have your helpers post the cards for each station after breakfast on Saturday. Arrange to have measuring devices or timers at each station. Use fitness activities that encourage improvement rather than competition such as:

• How flexible are you? Lie on the floor face down. Clasp your hands behind your neck and extend your elbows. See how far you can raise your chin off the floor. Practice this every day to see if you can improve.

• How strong are your legs? Jump as far as you can from this point. Jump three times. Think about what you did when you made your longest jump. Practice.

Check fitness resources such as *Everybody's a Winner: A Kid's Guide to New Sports and Fitness* by Tom Schneider (Little, Brown and Company) for similar tests of strength, speed, balance, agility or endurance.

Retreat Schedule

Friday

6:30 p.m.	Arrive and unpack
7 p.m.	Group singing
7:15 p.m.	Overdoser
7:30 p.m.	Session 1
8:30 p.m.	Break for a healthy snack
9 p.m.	Session 2

10 p.m.	Clothing scramble
11 p.m.	Prepare for bed
11:30 p.m.	Lights out

Saturday

7 a.m.	Wake-up call
8 a.m.	Breakfast
8:45 a.m.	Devotions
9 a.m.	Session 3
10 a.m.	Energy break
10:30 a.m.	Session 4
11:30 a.m.	Fitness stations
Noon	Lunch
1 p.m.	Free time
2:30 p.m.	Session 5
3:30 p.m.	Make a healthy choice
4:30 p.m.	Session 6
5:30 p.m.	Dinner
6:30 p.m.	How can I resist?
7:30 p.m.	Session 7
8:30 p.m.	Celebration
9:30 p.m.	Movie night
11 p.m.	Prepare for bed
11:30 p.m.	Lights out

Sunday

7 a.m.	Wake-up call
8 a.m.	Breakfast
8:45 a.m.	Devotions
9 a.m.	Session 8
10 a.m.	Closing worship
11 a.m.	Pack
11:30 a.m.	Lunch
12:30 p.m.	Leave for home

Retreat

Friday

Overdoser—(See Retreat for Youth and Parents, page 150.)

Session 1—(See page 12.)

Break for a healthy snack—Prepare apple and pear slices with peanut butter or cheese spread. Foods such as these taste good and emphasize the importance of healthy choices in diet.

Session 2—(See page 24.)

Clothing scramble—Bring a variety of jackets, hats, gloves and shoes. Pile all the clothing articles in the center of the floor and mix them up.

Have participants form teams of six and arrange themselves around the pile of clothing. Announce that this "Clothing scramble" is a way to focus on people's unique characteristics. Say: "When I say 'Go,' one member from each team should run to the pile and put on a jacket, a hat, gloves and shoes. None of these clothing articles can be his or her own. When the person is dressed completely, he or she must remove the same articles of clothing, run back to his or her team and tag the next person who repeats the process. The first team to finish will be first in line for breakfast."

Because of differences in sizes and styles of clothing, the combinations kids put on will bring lots of fun and laughter. Kids will see how different they can be, yet still a lot alike.

After the contest remind kids that no matter how different individuals are, it's still possible to appreciate one another's unique qualities. Have teams talk about the qualities unique to each person in the total group. For example, a team member may recognize an individual's ability to be a friend to everyone. Encourage participants to pick out qualities and abilities that set each person apart. After teams discuss the unique qualities of each person, they can get ready for bed.

Saturday

Devotions—Have kids form groups of four. Ask a volunteer to read 1 Corinthians 12:14-27. Give each person a piece of construction paper. Instruct kids to tear their paper into a shape that symbolizes the human body part they represent in their families, and have them tell why. For example, one person might tear his paper into the shape of an ear and explain that he always listens to everyone's problems.

After group members finish explaining, ask them to tape their symbols onto the wall. Close with a prayer that recognizes the unique value of each person. Pray that God will help the kids each to look at how their unique quality can help their family have good relationships with one another and with others outside the family.

Session 3—(See page 46.)

Energy break—Ask several of the most energetic kids to lead the group in exercises. Serve a nutritious snack such as fruit juice and granola bars.

Session 4—(See page 65.)

Fitness stations—Have kids choose a partner to go through the fitness stations you've prepared. The order of the stations shouldn't matter. Remind participants that the purpose of this activity isn't to see who's most physically fit, but to find out which areas individuals need to improve so they can glorify God with their bodies.

Lunch

Free time—Schedule different activities such as a volleyball tournament for the active kids and a croquet competition for those less active. Encourage those who prefer not to compete to go on a walk together. Make activities optional since some may choose to read or relax.

Session 5—(See page 80.)

Make a healthy choice—Give kids a choice of snacks. Have pop and candy bars at one end of a table and fruit juice with raw vegetables and yogurt dip at the other end. Place a sign, "Make a Healthy Choice," in the center of the table. Not all people will make a healthy choice, but you'll have made your point.

Session 6—(See page 98.)

Dinner

How can I resist?—Supply colored markers and give each person a one-pound coffee can and a piece of construction paper. On the construction paper, have kids each create a label for their cans to indicate who they are and what qualities they possess to help them avoid drug abuse. Ask kids to make sure their labels include:

- name and nicknames: How do others recognize you? (Richard, Dick, Flash)
- the manufacturer: Who made you who and what you are? (good family, friends and church)
- the brand: What are your outer qualities? (blond hair, green eyes, athletic physique)
- the ingredients: What are your inner qualities? (energetic, consistent, caring, thoughtful)

After kids complete their labels, have kids tape them onto their cans. Instruct kids to place their cans along one wall. Give each person a pencil and several small pieces of paper. Say: "Use the pencils and paper to write affirmations of one another's abilities to resist drug abuse. Write comments such as 'I'm impressed with your ability to say no to drugs, even to your best friend' or 'Your loyalty to your family members' expectations is great to see.' " If kids don't have time to write an affirmation for everyone, let them know the pencils and paper will remain available for the rest of the retreat.

Session 7—(See page 116.)

Celebration—Place magazines, construction paper, glue, masking tape, scissors and colored markers on a table. Give individuals each a balloon for each member of their family. Ask them to inflate their balloons and tie them to strings. Have kids write each family member's name on a balloon and decorate that balloon to represent that family member's healthy characteristics. Kids can cut out pictures, write words, make symbols or decorate the balloons any way they choose. When decorating is complete, have individuals meet in groups of four to explain the healthy characteristics each family member has and how those characteristics contribute to a positive family environment.

Then have kids tie the strings of their balloons together and tape them onto the wall. Encourage individuals to use the rest of the time to decorate the room for "Movie night." Have them make items such as paper chains or create posters about how to avoid drug abuse.

Movie night—Have kids form three groups. Have one group prepare popcorn and another group prepare drinks such as lemonade or fruit juice. Ask the third group to set up the videocassette recorder and TV set for the movie.

Play a fun video kids are familiar with. Stop the movie halfway through. Have the kids meet in three groups to create a new ending for the movie. Ask each group to perform its ending for the total group. After the performances, continue the movie.

Sunday

Devotions—Have a volunteer read aloud 1 John 4:7-12. Ask kids to discuss the following questions:

- What difference does it make when families realize that love comes from God?
- What evidences of God's love are present in your home?
- How do you share God's love with family members in your home?

• How can a relationship with God make a difference in your relationships with others outside the home?

After a brief discussion of these questions, ask each group member to say to the person on his or her right, "I see evidence of God's love in you by . . ." Close devotions with a prayer that God will help individuals use their godlike qualities to reach out to others in their struggles against drug abuse.

Session 8—(See page 134.)

Closing worship—Place a large bottle of cola and paper cups on a table in the center of the room. Ask kids to sit around the table.

Read aloud Psalm 139:13-18, 23-24. Say: "The Bible explains that God knows each of us intimately. He knows the inside and outside of who we are. He knows our joys and struggles.

"Because this cola contains caffeine, it can represent the struggle we have with drugs. It reminds us that every day we have the power to make wise or foolish choices about using drugs."

Pour a cup of cola for each kid and give it to him or her. After serving everyone, say: "What you do with this cup of cola is your choice. You may choose to pour it back into the bottle and crush your cup as a reminder that you'll have nothing to do with any drugs. Or you may choose to pour part of the cola back and drink the rest, acknowledging that caffeine is a safe drug, used in moderation. Keep the cup intact as a reminder of your commitment to make wise choices about using drugs. Think about how this cup of cola can symbolize the choice you make about using drugs. Tell your choice to one of the people next to you." Make sure everyone has someone to talk to.

Have kids stand in a circle and put their arms around one another as a symbol of support. Close the meeting with a prayer that God will help each person as he or she struggles with drug abuse. Thank God for his gifts of power and love, especially as they are expressed through others.

Remind kids to take home their cans with the affirmations to read and show their parents.

Resources

National organizations:

Alcohol and Drug Addiction Research Foundation (ARF)
33 Russell St.
Toronto, Ontario, Canada M5S 2S1
1-416-595-6111

Just Say No Foundation
1777 N. California Blvd., Ste. 210
Walnut Creek, CA 94596
1-800-258-2766

National Clearinghouse for Alcohol and Drug Information
Box 2345
Rockville, MD 20852
1-301-468-2600

National Council on Alcoholism, Inc.
12 W. 21st St., Ste. 700
New York, NY 10010
1-212-206-6770

National Federation of Parents for Drug-Free Youth (NFP)
8730 Georgia Ave., Ste. 200
Silver Spring, MD 20910
1-800-554-5437

Parents' Resource Institute for Drug Education (PRIDE)
100 Edgewood Ave., Ste. 1002
Atlanta, GA 30303
1-800-241-9746

Social Issues Resource Series:
Drugs, Alcohol
Box 2348
Boca Raton, FL 33427
1-800-327-0513

Students Against Driving Drunk (SADD)
Box 800
Marlboro, MA 01752
1-617-481-3568

The Wisconsin Clearinghouse
Box 1468
Madison, WI 53701
1-608-263-2797

Youth to Youth
700 Bryden Rd.
Columbus, OH 43215
1-614-224-4506

Cocaine Helpline
1-800-COCAINE

National Institute on Drug Abuse Hotline (NIDA)
1-800-662-HELP

National self-help groups:

Alcoholics Anonymous
Al-Anon and Alateen
Narcotics Anonymous
Families Anonymous
Adult Children of Alcoholics

(Refer to your telephone directory, or the directory of a large city, for information on the self-help groups meeting in your area. You may find additional alcohol and drug resources in your area.)

Bibliography

Ackerman, Robert J. *Children of Alcoholics: A Guidebook for Educators, Therapists and Parents*. Holmes Beach, FL: Learning Publications, 1983.

Alibrandi, Tom. *Young Alcoholics*. Minneapolis: CompCare Publications, 1978.

Black, Claudia. *My Dad Loves Me, My Dad Has a Disease*. Denver: M.A.C. Publishing, 1982.

Chemical Health: Prevention Ideas for Families, Schools and Communities. Anoka, MN: Minnesota Prevention Resource Center, 1979.

Consumer Reports Book Editors and Brecher, Edward M. *Licit and Illicit Drugs*. Boston: Little, Brown & Company, 1972.

Curran, Dolores. *Traits of a Healthy Family: Fifteen Traits Commonly Found in Healthy Families by Those Who Work With Them*. San Francisco: Harper & Row, Publishers, Inc., 1984.

Ezekoye, Stephanie, et al, eds. *Childhood and Chemical Abuse: Prevention and Intervention*. New York: The Haworth Press, Inc., 1986.

Frey, Diane and Carlock, Jesse C. *Enhancing Self-Esteem*. Muncie, IN: Accelerated Development Inc., 1984.

Goldstein, Arnold P., et al. *Skillstreaming the Adolescent: A Structured Learning Approach to Teaching Prosocial Skills*. Champaign, IL: Research Press, 1979.

Harrity, Anne and Cristensen, Ann. *Kids, Drugs and Alcohol: A Parent's Guide to Prevention and Intervention*. White Hall, VA: Betterway Publications, Inc., 1987.

Hulme, William and Hulme, Dale. *Who am I Lord . . . and Why Am I Here?* St. Louis, MO: Concordia Publishing House, 1984.

Jellinek, E.M. *The Disease Concept of Alcoholism*. New York: Hill House Publishers, 1960.

Johnson, Vernon E. *I'll Quit Tomorrow*. New York: Harper & Row, Publishers, Inc., 1980.

Lange, Arthur J. and Jakubowski, Patricia. *Responsible Assertive Behavior: Cognitive-Behavioral Procedures for Trainers*. Champaign, IL: Research Press, 1976.

McClelland, David C., et al. *The Drinking Man*. New York: Free Press, 1972.

Peele, Stanton and Brodsky, Archie. *Love and Addiction*. New York: Taplinger Publishing Company, Inc., 1975.

Polson, Beth and Newton, Miller. *Not My Kid: A Parent's Guide to Kids and Drugs*. New York: Arbor House Publishing Company, 1984.

Powell, John. *Why Am I Afraid to Tell You Who I Am?* Valencia, CA: Tabor Publishing, 1969.

Trobisch, Walter. *Love Yourself: Self-Acceptance and Depression*. Downers Grove, IL: InterVarsity Press, 1976.

Varenhorst, Barbara B. *Real Friends: Becoming the Friend You'd Like to Have*. San Francisco: Harper & Row, Publishers, Inc., 1983.

Wegsheider, Sharon. *Another Chance: Hope and Health for the Alcoholic Family*. Palo Alto, CA: Science and Behavior Books, Inc., 1980.

Weil, Andrew, M.D. and Rosen, Winifred. *Chocolate to Morphine: Understanding Mind-Active Drugs*. Boston: Houghton Mifflin Company, 1983.

What Works: Schools Without Drugs. Washington, DC: U.S. Department of Education, 1986.

Woititz, Janet G. *Adult Children of Alcoholics*. Pompano Beach, FL: Health Communications, Inc., 1983.

Training Volunteers in Youth Ministry

Video Kit

Give your volunteer youth workers a deeper understanding of youth ministry. You'll get expert, in-depth education with the **Training Volunteers in Youth Ministry** video kit. The nation's top authorities on teenagers and youth ministry provide solid, practical information.

Design a complete training program to meet your needs using helpful tips from the 128-page leaders guide and four 30-minute VHS videotapes . . .

Video 1: Youth Ministry Basics
Video 2: Understanding Teenagers
Video 3: Building Relationships
Video 4: Keys for Successful Meetings

You'll use this valuable resource again and again, sharpening the skills of your volunteer team. You'll discover how to find, motivate and keep volunteers. Plus, you'll strengthen your youth ministry team spirit with practical, affordable youth ministry training.

ISBN 0931-529-59-X, $98

Growing a Jr. High Ministry

by David Shaheen

Ministering to junior highers requires unique approaches and well-trained leaders. You'll find a wealth of practical ideas and suggestions for strengthening your ministry. Discover . . .

- Ministry-building leadership tips
- How junior highers think
- Ways to get parents involved
- How to build positive relationships

Plus, get scores of programming ideas for meetings, special events, discussion starters, attendance builders and more. Get proven help for your junior high ministry.

ISBN 0931-529-15-8, $12.95

Group's Best Jr. High Meetings, Vol. 1

Edited by Cindy Parolini

Save time with 58 of the best ready-to-use meetings from Group's JR. HIGH MINISTRY Magazine. You'll get complete meetings to help your young people . . .

- Develop self-esteem
- Build strong, positive friendships
- Improve decision-making skills
- Communicate with parents and more

Your young people will love lively meetings packed with activities, games and Bible studies. Create an encouraging time of growth for your junior highers with faith-building programs.

ISBN 0931-529-58-1, $18.95

Look for these exceptional youth ministry resources at your local Christian bookstore. Or order direct. Write Group Books, Box 481, Loveland, CO 80539. Add $2.50 ($4.00 for video orders) postage and handling to your order. Colorado residents add 3% sales tax.